JOE ESTEVEZ:
WIPING OFF THE "SHEEN"

BY **BRAD PAULSON**
AND **CHRIS WATSON**

Published in the USA by:

BEARMANOR MEDIA
P.O. BOX 71426
ALBANY, GEORGIA 31708
www.BearManorMedia.com

ISBN-10: 1-59393-281-2 (alk. paper)
ISBN-13: 978-1-59393-281-7 (alk. paper)

Printed in the United States of America.

COVER DESIGNED BY DREW MARTIN

BOOK DESIGN AND LAYOUT BY VALERIE THOMPSON

TABLE OF CONTENTS

"Joe is one of the most talented, creative, and best friends I have."

—ACTOR ROBERT Z'DAR

"It's always a pleasure to work with the great Joe Estevez. Joe's a good friend."

—ACTOR CONRAD BROOKS

"I can't tell you how much I have enjoyed my friendship and working relationship with Joe over so many years. The work we do as actors can be a hard slog at times, but when you get to do your thing with such a professional as Joe, suddenly it becomes fun as well. He has always been the consummate performer, always giving and so kind to his fellow actors. And what a body of work. Hey, in my mind, the guy is a legend. We should all be so lucky to share a set with Joe Estevez."

—ACTOR RICHARD NORTON

"Joe is an incredibly underrated actor. The right director who gives him a chance will be rewarded."

—ACTOR/DIRECTOR DUANE WHITAKER

"My friend Joe is one of the best kept secrets in Hollywood—a great actor but even more important, an amazing human being. I heard his family is trying to get into the biz—it's hard to follow an act like Joe!"

—ACTOR/DIRECTOR DAVID HEAVENER

"The best way to convince me to do a movie is to say 'Joe Estevez is in it' and I'm there. Joe is the most lovable rogue I know—both on and off screen. We've worked together in a half-dozen films and Joe has the unique talent of bringing out the best performance in everybody who works with him. I always look forward with relish to our next collaboration."

—ACTOR/DIRECTOR JAY RICHARDSON

INTRODUCTION

Joe Estevez is, without a doubt, the biggest name in the world of independent cinema. He has appeared in more feature films than virtually any other actor in history. Though he has carved out an everlasting name for himself in this realm of the filmmaking industry, he is much more than simply an indie film actor. Joe Estevez is a consummate theatre actor, who continually returns to the stage. He is a highly established voiceover artist, whose voice can frequently be heard narrating commercials and documentaries. Plus, some people forget, he is an actor who has appeared in numerous A-level feature films, several television series, and a number of movies of the week.

Joe Estevez's place in cinematic history has been cast to stone by his movies being broadcast and discussed on such iconic television shows as USA's *Up All Night* and *Mystery Science Theater*. But, more than his movies simply being shown on programs that devote themselves to the more abstract creations in the world of modern cinema; movies he has starred in have also been broadcast on such respected networks as HBO and Showtime, where they have devoted entire days to featuring his films. Thus, Joe Estevez sits at a level that few film actors will ever experience.

When the author asked me to write the introduction for his book, I was excited and more than happy to do so. Having worked with Joe several times, in addition to having come to know him personally, I have nothing but the highest regard for the man and his acting skills. Though there is no better person to better describe the life and times of Joe Estevez than the man himself—as will be witnessed within the pages of this book—readers may find it interesting to view a few stories from his life on the set, via the

Scott Shaw with Joe in *Toad Warrior.*
Courtesy of Scott Shaw.

perspective of someone who has acted with and directed him in feature films virtually since the point in history when he set his course on becoming the biggest indie film actor in the world—or, as I like to title him, "An indie film demigod." To this end, allow me to tell a few tales about my interaction with the man. From this, it may come to be understood what an outstanding performer Joe Estevez truly is.

I first met Joe when Donald G. Jackson and I were creating the film *The Roller Blade Seven* in 1991. A casting director suggested Joe to us. He was recommended due to the fact that our contract with our executive producer detailed that we needed to add "Name talent" to the production. We had already worked with Academy Award nominee and Golden Globe winner Karen Black and Clint Eastwood co-stars Don Stroud and William Smith, plus the brother of "Rocky," Frank Stallone. Though each of these actors brought a unique element to the film, we still needed someone to complete the production and tie all of the elements of the story together. This person was to become Joe Estevez.

The fact of the matter was, Don Jackson and I had both been a fan of the film *Soultaker* (1990), in which Joe starred. When his name was suggested to us, and we found out we could actually add him to our cast, we were both excited to meet the man and to work with him.

On the evening of our first scheduled shoot date, we awaited Joe's arrival, as our crew lighted our stages at the Hollywood Center building on Hollywood Boulevard in Hollywood, California. An interesting side note is that we had taken over the offices that Quentin Tarantino had used while producing his directorial debut, *Reservoir Dogs* (1992). Though he had only used the office suite for formal production activities, we had set up stages and sets in the building.

Due to the fact that Joe was an established actor, we assumed that he would have a certain attitude—as most actors in his position possess. As such, we had a private waiting room set up for him where he could relax and do all the things that a "name actor" would do while they awaited their call to the set.

Joe arrived. Introductions were made and we directed him to his room. But Joe would have nothing to do with it. All he did was joke about the fact that we even had such a room for him. Instead, Joe sat down on the set, as preparations took place, and he laughed and joked with Don Jackson and myself. He was completely different than we expected and was nothing but an absolutely unassuming, nice guy.

As has been well documented in many other venues, *The Roller Blade Seven* has become a quite talked about, often criticized, long-standing cult film classic. In actuality, it became the first "Zen Film." What this means is, it became the first film that was made in the Zen Filmmaking tradition. The reason I mention this is at the heart of Zen Filmmaking is the fact that we never use a screenplay to create a film. In the case of *The Roller Blade Seven*, Don wanted to use two books I had written, entitled *Essence* and *Time*, as the basis for the majority of the dialogue that made up the film. These books were made up of spiritual aphorisms. Some actors took to this style of film creation immediately, while others did not. In the case of Joe, he loved it. He looked through the books, found the phrases he wanted to say, and he was off...From his exacting talents as an actor, he spoke the aphorisms with total conviction and established his character as the diabolical Saint Offender. In association with the words from the two books, we guided him through a few story points and "Saint Offender" created the basis for the entire storyline of the film and its sequel, *Return of the Roller Blade Seven* (1992), which we shot back-to-back with the primary feature.

Luckily, we were allowed to work with Joe more than once during the creation of these films. On our way to a daytime shoot at Bronson Cave, the location used as the Bat Cave for the 1960s television series *Batman*, as well as having been used in numerous other films and televisions projects, we stopped off to grab some lunch at a deli located in a supermarket on Franklin Avenue in Hollywood. While we waited for our lunch to be prepared, Joe and I sat around looking at the newly arrived *Hollywood Reporter* and studying the various film productions listed near the end of the publication. As Joe and I were both working on a few different projects at the time, he jokingly asked me, "Whose name is listed more? Yours or mine?" We looked and without a doubt his name was listed many more times than mine. It was then that I realized that he had set the stage for the future of his career—to become the biggest name in the history of the independent film.

After lunch, we made our way to Bronson Cave. We were to shoot several scenes. Arguably most important was a scene where Joe and I did sword combat. As a lifelong martial artist I am always initially concerned when interacting, on a combat level, with another actor. First of all, I hope that their techniques will sell for the camera and, secondarily, I am always cautious that they will not hurt me or I will not hurt them if they do not possess the developed theatrical combat skills to make a fight scene work for the camera. This, combined with the fact that I was the producer of the film, and as 16mm film production is expensive, I wanted to shoot as few takes as possible to keep production costs down. So, I initially held a small amount of concern as we entered our locations and began to shoot our scenes.

Another essential element of Zen Filmmaking is that we do not do long, involved, and oftentimes boring choreography sessions. So, all the fight and weapon scenes are shot pretty much off the cuff. In the case of this day's shoot, Don and the assistant cameraman loaded the camera with film, as I spoke to Joe about a few of my ideas about our sword action. Again, the moment we began filming, I was nothing but impressed with Joe's professionalism. His sword-play and his onscreen persona were outstanding. The scenes were shot effortlessly and they looked great!

On our final day of shooting with Joe, on the *Roller Blade Seven*, we returned to our stages at the Hollywood Center Building. Though we did several scenes, and some of them did not even involve Joe, he was nothing but patient and full of humor. Whereas many established actors expect the entire shoot day to revolve around them when they are on the set, this is not the case with Joe. He patiently

Joe and Scott swordfight. Courtesy of Scott Shaw.

and happily sat around speaking to the attractive, scantily-clad Asian girl that we would later eat food off of in one of the scenes of the film. He did this while Don, our crew, and I worked on other scenes from our jail set.

Perhaps the most telling thing about the true talent of Joe Estevez is his command of theatrical improv. I believe this is the true test of an actor. I first encountered his skills while filming *Return of the Roller Blade Seven*. There is an uncut scene in the movie that goes on for twenty minutes where Joe's character, "Saint Offender," and Don's character, "Reverend Donaldo," talk about the abstract elements of life and spirituality. The scene ends with a great exchange of ongoing "Fuck you's." With no coaching whatsoever, Joe sat down and went head-to-head with "Reverend Donaldo," and the scene was great! Any film historian would be awestruck to find out that it was unscripted and completely performed via improvisational acting.

Another tribute to Joe Estevez, the actor: On that same evening, Joe was happy to get on the dance floor with myself and several of our starlets as we completed one of the most bizarre elements of the film, where the cast members enter into an abstract world of, for lack of a better term, a disco dance-off. Joe shook his hips with the best of 'em!

By the end of filming *The Roller Blade Seven* my admiration for the acting craft of Joe Estevez was set. We worked together again on such films as *Max Hell Frog Warrior* a.k.a. *Toad Warrior* (1996), *Guns of El Chupacabra* (1997), *Hitman City* (2003), and *Vampire Blvd* (2004). I would be remiss if I did not mention the true professionalism of Joe and his mastery of acting that he brought to the set for each of these films. He would arrive on the set with absolutely no idea about what was to take place and proceed to lay down incredible, improvisational performances, with only the smallest amount of guidance.

I believe one of the greatest elements of Joe Estevez and a true testament to his acting ability is the fact that no matter whether he is working on a very high-budget production or one that has a very small production budget, the man always brings his A-game to the set. Whereas many established actors, with a long list of credits similar to those of Joe, would never think about being a part of a small budget film, Joe is always happy to be on the set, bringing not only his unique look but his highly refined command of acting technique to each and every performance he is a part of.

In closing, Joe Estevez is a true creature of Hollywood. Not only does he live in the filmmaking capital of the world, but he can also be found speaking with his fans and his friends at the various hangouts around the city. There has been many an occasion that I have decided to stop at a Starbucks, Coffee Bean, or some other restaurant in Hollywood and there he would be, Joe Estevez, sitting and enjoying a coffee and telling the tales of his life. He never puts on an air of superiority, as do so many established Hollywood actors. Instead, he is forever the nicest guy you will ever want to meet.

SCOTT SHAW

FOREWORD

Joe in *Mob Daze*.

I was working on my first movie. I was the producer/co-writer/co-star of the film. It was a small, independent film. The script got good reviews from everyone and attracted a few people that I think would have turned it down otherwise. One of those people was Joe Estevez. Joe did that movie because of the script and the character he got to play—a drunk lawyer who is also the uncle of one of the main characters.

I bring this relatively unknown film up for a few reasons. First, it was my first time meeting Joe. I learned quickly that he was a friendly guy who could get along with anyone. Second, Joe showed up on set and changed the whole atmosphere. By that time the cast knew we had a bad director behind the camera and on a low-budget shoot you need a genius. Joe showed up and changed the gloom hanging over the cast into a group that was having a blast. The fun didn't come from drinking or partying, but just from Joe's personality—he was infectious. The shoot was a few days from finishing so Joe inadvertently sent everyone home feeling much better about the experience than they would have otherwise.

The last reason is simple. There was one showing of this film. As a co-writer I was on the edge of my seat listening. There were a moderate amount of laughs. David Lawson and I wrote the script our first year of college so I wasn't too surprised. About halfway through the movie I learned a big lesson as a writer—YOU'RE ONLY AS GOOD AS YOUR ACTORS. Joe Estevez burst through the courtroom door and LOUD laughter ensued from beginning to end. Joe went above and beyond with the script. The movie may have been so-so, but Joe was hilarious.

I enjoyed working with Joe so much that I made sure he was in the next movie I worked on. The shoot was a bit insane—a feature in eight days with a rookie director (me) behind the camera. Joe was brought in on one of the last days of filming. I teamed Joe up with a legendary actor. There was a lot of excitement in the air—actors who complained about working too much were coming to set even though they weren't needed. When everyone was on set, I discovered a few things. First, the legendary actor couldn't stand—he was supposed to have several fight scenes. Second, the same actor had a severe memory problem. He had no idea what was in the script. As Joe and this actor rehearsed, it became evident the guy couldn't remember any of it five minutes later. As a rookie director, it was a nightmare. We only had the location for a short amount of time, and there was no way I could afford the location or actors another day. Joe and I talked about it briefly. He suggested he get the gist of it and see what happens. We set up to shoot with me thinking we didn't have a shot. "Action!"

I don't know how to describe it other than to say it was absurd and amazing at the same time. Joe minimized what both actors were supposed to say and weaved it into a hilarious set of scenes. On the last day of filming, Joe got an ovation. To cut to the chase, Joe saved my backside. I wasn't sure how audiences would react. We toured with that movie and the scenes with Joe always got laughs. They are the scenes people talk to me about the most (usually following "Estevez was hilarious" is "Why doesn't the other guy stand up?").

Joe and I have several mutual friends, acquaintances, and co-workers. I have never met someone who doesn't love Joe. He's professional, fun to be around, and is very down to earth. While Joe is more associated with cult films, people forget he's done many other projects. You might notice that the films Joe talks about being proudest of are dramas and comedies. A lot of them never came out (typical in the world of independent film, a producer won't give up the rights to their movie unless they're guaranteed x amount—as a producer I can tell you I have never seen a dime that I didn't get up front). It's a shame that some of the performances Joe is proudest of sit on someone's shelf. It's more of a shame that people zero in on a few movies over an entire filmography. Joe has worked with everyone from Gene Hackman to Tonya Harding. He has acted in well over 200 films. I hope anyone reading this book will appreciate the career of Joe Estevez the way I do. Many scoff at actors making 20 million on a big Hollywood movie. We wonder when they'll do something independent, something that requires acting. If you want a real actor, here's your chance to meet Joe Estevez. Look at his films and you will find that Joe has played every type of character imaginable. Despite being in 200-plus films it is difficult to find any one performance like another. Joe is a true chameleon, able to put himself into whatever character you throw at him. Joe Estevez is a living, breathing definition of what a true actor is.

CHRIS WATSON

WHY I LOVE JOE ESTEVEZ

Evil Ever After
cast photo.

There are many reasons to love Joe Estevez. He has hundreds of movies to his credit on IMDb. He's an international star (he's made movies in twelve different countries). He's acted with the likes of everyone from Dustin Diamond (*Saved By the Bell* [1989]) to Robert Z'Dar (*Tango and Cash* [1989]) to Jack Palance to Gene Hackman. He filled in for his brother on one of the greatest movies of all time, *Apocalypse Now* (1979). And even though a lot of people know of his stature in the independent film scene, few are aware he's an excellent playwright as well.

Recently, I had the pleasure of seeing a staged reading of a couple plays he had written, *Hobos* and *Pizza Man*, and was highly impressed at the quality and intelligence in his work. As I've told Joe before, he has a great deal of street cred in the indie film community and is often referred to as an underrated and highly talented actor. The best thing about Joe to me, though, is he's a genuine, compassionate human being. In a town like Los Angeles, a place known for its flakes and divas, Joe shines apart. He's the type of guy who makes you feel like you've been lifelong friends after only hanging out a few times. And regardless of some of the classic films and people he's been involved with, he's not a diva or name dropper. He's approachable and friendly.

Mostly though, it's Joe's larger-than-life personality that fascinates me. He's filled with a childlike exuberance that floods every room he enters. This is a man who truly enjoys every second he's alive. He appreciates life in a way many people sadly never will. As you'll read in his interview Joe's faced desperation, hard times and fierce opposition. Yet, he's overcome and refused to give up. The result of which is an incredibly prolific and rewarding career which he's carved a grand niche for himself.

One look in his eyes and you see a man who has faced his demons and overcome. Joy and zest for life have taken the wheel and are here to stay. I saw a perfect example of this the first time I met Joe in a restaurant for lunch. Every single staff member at the place knew his name and he knew theirs. Interacting with them, from the management to the busboys, it is as if they were all great friends. When I saw Joe spending so much time talking to one busboy in particular, it brought a smile to my face. This is what I love so much about Joe: he cares about the little guy. He will show you the same amount of respect whether you are an Oscar-winning film-maker or a bum on the street. He will go out of his way to not only give you the time of day but make sure you are acknowledged. I have never seen an actor go so far out of their way to commune with their fellow man before I met Joe. He as a person has something we as a country desperately need: a deep regard and respect for human life.

Of all the time I've spent with Joe, I've never felt like he's had an agenda. I never felt like he was trying to get something out of me. He would be just as content negotiating a business deal as he would eating at Sizzler. Despite the impressive number of movies and people he's worked with, Joe doesn't have a stigma about being with the "in" crowd. He's not about the trends, fashions and all the other Hollywood bullshit that comes with it. He simply loves people. He loves talking to, spending time with and learning about them.

When my grandfather on my father's side of the family passed away, my father told me something about him that really stuck in my head. He said, "Your grandfather is the type of man who can talk to a stranger in a store for a half an hour about anything. In fact, lots of times, it was more than an hour and a half." I remember being very endeared by this; thinking that this was such a wonderful trait to have: to be able to strike up a conversation with a stranger about anything. To have a truly good time and make people happy wherever you go. This is exactly what Joe is like. Not only does he bring his childlike exuberance into a room with him, he leaves it there long after he's gone. Joe's the kind of guy people want to be around. When I'm around someone like that, who is so full of love for life and so kind to those around him, my pessimism dulls and I regain my faith in humanity.

I am a better person having a friend like Joe and I am honored that Chris Watson asked me to write this book with him. Joe is one of the greatest gifts and friends an independent filmmaker can have and hopefully people will realize after reading this just what an amazing person and actor he is and hire him for their movies. Watson and I won't be content until we see Joe on every billboard on the Sunset Strip.

BRAD PAULSON

Interview with Joe Estevez

Let's go back to the beginning. Tell us where you were born, raised, etc.

I was the last of twelve children from immigrant parents. My father was from Spain, my mother was from Ireland. My uncle Michael Phelan was a very famous actor in Dublin. He was one of the charter members of the Abbey Theatre. He was also a revolutionist. He was one of the IRA men that held the post office from the British in Dublin for three days during what was the Easter Rising in 1916. He was sentenced to death and because the British had executed an American before him, the United States got up in arms. So, they stopped executing revolutionists, but he spent an awful lot of time in prison. After I was a professional actor for about three or four years, I had changed my name to Phelan just in honor of my Uncle Michael. If you go on my IMDb Joe Phelan has a pretty good career for about five years, then he just disappears off the face of the map. I went back to my original name because, as much as I admire my uncle Michael Phelan, that's not who I am. I'm Joe Estevez and I should act under the name of Joe Estevez. That's the name my father gave me.

How many siblings do you have?

I have eight brothers and one sister.

Can you tell us a little about your relationship with your brother, Martin Sheen?

In regards to my brother Ramon Estevez, better known under his stage name Martin Sheen, back in the day when we were kids he was six, seven years older than I am. He was at that age that, of all my brothers, I looked up to him. I looked up to him far and away more because he was so charismatic. He was so courageous. In Dayton, where we grew up, he was considered a terrific actor. There was a local show there called *The Rising Generation*. He went on and did a reading. If he won, he'd go on to the national, big show. He won that and a free trip to New York. At 16, he was like the biggest star in Dayton, Ohio. He was such a charismatic guy that I really looked up to him—I wanted to be like him. I admired his qualities as a human being. I remember him going off to New York when he was 18. I was 12 and my brother John was 15. We made him one of these good luck things. We went down to the train station and watched him board the train and go off to New York. We were behind him one hundred percent. All of the people on Brown Street were behind him and wanted him to do well. I felt in my heart that day that Ramon Estevez left—he never really came home again. He became international. He didn't belong to Dayton anymore. He belonged to the world. That's just a natural thing to happen. I understand that totally. When I cast my dye to be an actor, he got me that audition in *The Story of Pretty Boy Floyd* (1974). I did that gig and remember him telling me, "Whenever I work, kid, you're going to work." I was very instrumental in getting him the job in *California Kid* (1974). Then, that was it. He got me the audition but my brother was never comfortable with me being an actor. I do not know why. That is something you would have to ask him. As close as I thought we were when we were growing up, we have never been close since I decided to become a professional actor. I do not know who this guy Martin Sheen is. He seems like a good guy. He has done a lot of good, but he is not the Ramon Estevez I grew up with in Dayton, Ohio.

What was the situation with the NRA commercials?

I was approached to do a voiceover for the National Rifle Association. I really went over in my mind whether I should do this or not. Along with this, they were paying a pretty good paycheck and that was

Joe Estevez as Meeks in *Bunyan* © **Picture Show Partners L.P. All Rights Reserved.**

part of why I decided to do it. I'm not a Democratic or Republican, I'm an Independent. I was watching how the Democrats were manipulating the NRA and blaming them for all the crime, all the madness that goes on in this country. In a lot of countries, it is against the law to not have a gun. It's not the gun that's the problem— it's the madness behind the gun. The conclusion I came to in my mind was that in going after the NRA, it wasn't going after the real problem. The real problem was how we raise our children. It's the garbage on TV and how violence is displayed. It's how parents are very lazy with their children. The parents often promote violence themselves. We are a very, incredibly, violent society. I saw that the Democratic Party was going after an easy fix by blaming it on the NRA and not addressing the real problem. That's why I did those ads, which were terrific ads by the way. When they played on TV, somebody called and told my brother, "Hey, that guy sounds like you!" My brother had a press conference on national TV and said, "My brother, poor sap, doesn't know what he was talking about and he was duped into doing this ad." I had no platform that I could speak from. I couldn't call a press conference and have the networks and newspapers show up. I had nothing. I went on an entertainment show and said, "You've got to promise me; I'll do your show but please do not edit what I'm saying." Well, of course, they edited what I said. I didn't come out looking like a complete fool, but what it said and what it was edited for me to say were two different messages. They still won't do you live. They'll do you on tape so they can have their way with the tape. After that, if you're in a hole stop digging. I'm not going to do anymore of these celebrity TV shows. Not surprisingly, *Time* magazine ripped me apart, *L.A. Times* ripped me apart, but surprisingly the one paper that really stood up for me was *Variety*. They said, "Wait a minute. Look at this guy. This guy has done a helluva lot of movies. This guy has got a marvelous body of work. This guy hasn't ever caused any trouble. He's never been arrested. He doesn't beat his wife. He hasn't been caught in any whorehouses. He's not out there doing drugs. This is a real, regular, straight-shooter and he says what he believes in his heart." I really appreciated that the show-business magazine actually stood up for me. After I was crucified out there, I called my brother a year later and said, "I want to tell you, I'm going to do another ad." He said, "Oh, that's fine, I don't care. Geez, I shouldn't have said anything about it in the first place." It was as if it didn't mean anything to him. He didn't realize how much it crushed and how much work it cost me from the industry that was looking at me like I'm some kind of ass. That hurt. That hurt my career, credibility, and me as a husband and father and brother. To have my family and friends read that about me and having no recourse to answer that. That's still a sore point—sadness with me that I carry. I don't think that my brother has the foggiest how much damage he did with it.

Why do you think Martin changed his name instead of using the Estevez name?

The story is he was a New York actor and not that he had anything against Puerto Ricans, but in New York there's a Puerto Rican connotation to the name Estevez, so he wanted a very white-bred name. Very few people remember a bishop by the name of Bishop Fulton J. Sheen. He was very dramatic. He had a TV show on Sunday night and he'd come out in these marvelous robes, these bishop robes, and this incredible lighting and he'd do a half-hour sermon. My brother was very religious, very Catholic, and he was taken with Bishop Fulton J. Sheen. So, he got the Sheen name from Fulton J.

Sheen and he got the Martin from Strother Martin. At least, that's the story that's going around this week anyway.

I think everybody gets confused because Emilio keeps the last name Estevez and Charlie keeps the last name Sheen. But it was all originally the last name Estevez?

Yeah. Nobody, I think, has ever changed their name legally. As a matter of fact, I think he got stopped on a plane because he didn't have the Estevez identification.

When I was growing up and I saw *Young Guns* (1988), I thought that Emilio Estevez and Charlie Sheen had two different fathers.

Yeah, that makes sense, but no. They're full brothers, Charlie and Emilio.

Did you come from an acting background?

Not really. There was just my uncle. My father was a factory worker. We were raised to be factory workers. Back then if children got an education then got a job in a factory, parents had done their duty. So, I got a high-school education. I got my girlfriend pregnant, I went into the Navy. I got out of the Navy with a readymade family and got a job in a factory and stayed there for quite awhile and all the while wanting to act, but it just seemed like a distant dream. I started doing theatre constantly and I would do one play after another and while I was in rehearsal for one play, I'd be on the boards for another. I think actually when I was in the factory, I worked more as an actor; I did more acting, per se, than I had done at any other time in my life. I mean, I think it literally just saved my life. I had a lot of trouble with John Barleycorn calling me. The booze...and I think that if I was in that factory without being able to perform, there was no hope for my life. I'm looking at forty years of factory work and ending up just a total mess, an alcoholic.

When did you first become interested in pursuing an acting career?

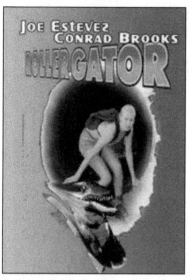

Rollergator **cover.** Courtesy of Scott Shaw.

My brother got me an audition out here for a movie called *The Story of Pretty Boy Floyd* (1974). It was a TV movie and I had known the director, Clyde Ware. So, I came out here to audition for that. And I thought, at the time, film was kind of artificial. I thought real actors were stage actors and I still believe myself to be a stage actor. But I came out here, auditioned for *The Story of Pretty Boy Floyd*. I got the job and I got my SAG card. I went back to Ohio. I worked for another three months in the factory and then came out here with the money I got from that gig. I was able to get a foothold. I was able to get first and last month's rent and the rest, as they say, is history. When I got here I still did quite a bit of stage. I auditioned with 400 other male actors and got the part in a play called *Echoes*. It was in that Pasadena Playhouse that reopened; the Pasadena Playhouse in 1980. I was always doing stage readings in and around this town and still I do stage readings whenever I have the opportunity. I just wrote two stage plays that I want to do in Ireland. Two years ago, my very good friend Nick Hardin and I toured Ireland with a play called *A Short Wake* for six weeks. I get on the stage as much as I possibly can, but you can't make a living at theatre. I mean, the most you're going to get is four hundred dollars a week, which is tough to live on and that's if you got a lead. You have to have some kind of TV series or something. Not impossible, but tough. So I came here to Los Angeles and settled in, my wife and I. The next film I did, after *The Story of Pretty Boy Floyd*, was with a gentleman by the name of Bruce Morgan. I'm only bringing him up because I am going to do a movie with him in September with Margaret O'Brien. She's an Academy Award winner. She and Bill Smith, who was our best man, by the way.

The father of "Conan" was your best man?

Yes, and *Rich Man, Poor Man* (1976) and *Hawaii Five-0*, and has been nominated himself, but he was the best man at our wedding and I was best man at his wedding.

How did your wife handle your decision to become an actor?

I have to apologize. My first wife's name is Vicky. We were married for 13 years. I said I was coming out here to start a new life and be a professional actor. She never once resisted that. She was totally all for it. I came out here in February. She brought my oldest daughter out, drove across the country leaving her friends, parents, and life behind to join me. She helped me with my dream. I don't think our marriage was ever one made in heaven, it was a rocky marriage. But I look back on it now; she was just a regular gal. She was used to Dayton, Ohio, and her friends. She wasn't ready for all the back slapping and the showbiz kind of bravado. She was a bashful, small-town girl. She really wasn't the type of personality that could handle that in a marriage that was already on a rocky road. It just helped us come apart and I was part of Hollywood, trying to make it. The friends I was making were intimidating to her. She felt very uncomfortable going with me to different affairs or even coming to the set. She was just bashful. It made us grow further apart until the marriage broke up. My second wife divorced me, but I was the one that divorced Vicky. If we had stayed in Dayton, I'm sure the scenario would have been much different. I've often felt bad about that. She stuck her neck out for me and all she got is a divorce for it and child support. It's one of the things I'm not real proud of, but I think if she ever reads this book I want her to know, "I'm sorry it worked out this way. Thank you for having the faith in me to come out here and take this chance with me." When you're younger, I think people are more disposable. You don't consider their emotions when you've got your eye on that prize. I hurt my former wife, I see that now. I'm sorry for it. I feel bad about it. If I was as mature then as I am now, I would have done it differently. I don't know if it would have come to the same end or not, but I would've done it differently. I would have been more caring. I would have been more of a man about it. Of course, the John Barleycorn gets in the way. I feel bad about it.

What kind of training have you had and do you think it's worth it or is it instinctual?

I think Marlon Brando and James Dean and all these great actors out of the '50s would have been great actors no matter what they did. I'll try to be gentle here as far as acting schools go. I taught for awhile in an acting school. I was into teaching a way of life as an actor. I was into teaching the spirit of what one has to have about themselves to make a living, to persevere, and to survive in this profession. Not only to survive, but to prosper in this profession. Not only so much materially, but mainly spiritually as a human being—to grow spiritually as a human being through acting. I never believed really in the art of acting. I believe it's a minor art. I think my wife is an artist, that's a much higher art form than acting.

How do you view yourself as an actor?

I don't consider myself better than thou because I'm an actor. I just love being an actor and that's why I do it. If I loved digging ditches, I would dig ditches and that would be my art form. A lot of people would come to this acting school and all acting schools throughout Hollywood and they would have misgivings about what it is to be an actor and forget acting. They came out here to be celebrities and had no idea what the actual craft, art of acting, is, and I don't think that's something you can teach. I think that's something that's born in your heart and it lives there. It's not there by accident and you can cultivate this art. The best way to cultivate this art as an actor is to do it, the same way as a filmmaker is to do it. You're going to learn a lot more from the mistakes you make while making a film than you are by a professor telling you how you're going to do this and grading you. They don't grade you on a film; you grade yourself on a film. If you said what you wanted to say then it's a good film. If it doesn't, you try again until it says something you want to say.

Why did you decide to stop teaching?

I stopped teaching because I thought I was taking these kids'

Peter Whittaker and Joe Estevez. Shot by Steve Thompson, © Brett Kelly.

money under false pretenses. I didn't want to give them false hope and a lot of these kids had no hope. They had no chance of ever getting a job as an actor. Now, Hollywood's a different beast. With reality shows, with the singing shows, we are growing celebrities here more than talent. I think that for that type of breeding ground, for someone that wants to, excuse me, show their ass and they got the chutzpah to get out there and show their ass regardless of what people think about them, than this is the town to do that. I don't know what Paris Hilton is famous for...giving head in an X-rated porn film and really that's how she got up, but back in the day if you did a *Playboy* that was the end of your career. Now, if you get a spread in *Penthouse*, that's a boost to your career. So, I think this whole Hollywood ideology about making stars and such, I think it's changed quite a bit. I'm old school. If there was no such thing as film I would still be an actor because that's what I am. That's what I am. The only thing is that now as I'm getting old that passion, that compassion that I have in myself, it's the best tool that I have to serve the kind of heart that I have as a human being. I used to work with an old circus performer. He said, "You know, in the circus, we always gave a performance, but we always took a bow." I never forgot that. You want to see circus performances, man it's an art, when they take a bow. As an actor, my wife knows this, you know this, and you give a performance. You give of yourself and your spirit. You give that. You put it out there, you know. That audience does what they will. They trample you or they can praise you, but to put yourself out there is humanity as Shakespeare says, "We tread the stage." I don't want to do *Hamlet* right now, but that was my philosophy as an actor which I'm still so passionate about.

I love actors like my friend Ed Asner, who is acting in my two plays. One's called *Hobos* and one's called *Pizza Man*. I'm gonna get Ed Asner and Scott Wilson to do the reading from these plays, but I admire Ed Asner. He's got two incredible big hits out there in the last year or so. He's got more money than he can ever spend. We did a play with the two of those guys called *Uranium and Peaches* by Peter Cook. We did three different staged readings around town in a ten-year period. Scott's a very, very giving actor. I think the best actors are the giving actors, but there's also selfish actors. When I first met Erik Estrada, he was a very selfish actor. He was king of the world on *CHiPs*. Ten years after I first worked with him on *CHiPs*, I met him again on another project and he was a totally giving, beautiful, beautiful man. He just changed. He had a motorcycle accident in those years between the *CHiPs* years and when I saw him again. I don't want to cast dispersions on Erik Estrada, because he's a super guy, but he was a selfish man back in the day. But now, he's an actor. He's in it. He's learned Spanish. He didn't know Spanish [before]. He learned Spanish to go to Mexico to do soap operas to keep working. These guys don't make anything. At least here he's got a name, but these Mexican soap opera actors make very little.

What are the odds, realistically for someone to come out here and make a living as an actor?

I think, if they're not deceiving themselves and they are actors, the more that you believe in yourself the better chance. The old adage I would tell these kids was that God did not put this desire in your heart to be an actor by mistake. It's for you to have more faith than you have in that and the more you act on that faith, the more

Joe performing with Ed Asner.

successful you're going to be. Not that you are going to be a matinee idol, but that you will make a living. I have made a living as an actor for over 35 years. It has always taken care of me. Back when I was married to this one woman, I had a small carpet-cleaning company called Actor's Dry Cleaning Company: "Out Damned Spot" was our motto. Anyway, I let this business die purposely. I was actually getting a lot of customers because this dry-cleaning carpet thing actually worked pretty good. But I let it die purposely because if I started depending of this money I was making I would back off on the acting, so I let it die a fast, quick death and said this is where my financial future lies.

When you quit your job, what did you have to sacrifice before you became a professional actor full time?

You know, in 1972, I took a leave of absence from the factory. Three months. I tried to come out here to get a foothold. Couldn't do it, so I went back to the factory for two years until I got that audition for *The Story of Pretty Boy Floyd*. I gave up nothing. I gave up misery, want, and doubt. When I committed myself to be an actor it opened up the world to me—before that I was hiding from the world. When I left the factory, I took a three month's leave of absence. If I had quit the factory then I would have had no choice. I would have had to make it out here. And because I had to have made it, I would have made it. But I always knew I could go back. And so I did go back. A second time I quit so there was no going back. I think it's because back in Dayton, Ohio, I was getting all the leads. It was about six or seven theatres in town. Community theatres. I would just go from one to the other, picking the play I would want to do and I would get leads in them and I'd be the big fish in the small pond. I was cock of the walk in Dayton, Ohio. But I hadn't committed to this as my life as what I needed to do. I think I could have left at any time. And I had that problem with John Barleycorn calling. Booze.

What did alcohol do to your career at that time?

When I first came out here, I was in the big arena. I was doing auditions with people I'd seen on TV and I was incredibly intimidated. I thought, "Oh my God, these guys, they must be great and I'm just this amateur actor from Dayton." Of course, you can take care of that with a little bottle of courage. John Barleycorn, you're right up there with them. When I first came out here, it hurt me dearly. I remember reading drunk for *One Flew Over the Cuckoo's Nest* (1975). I remember reading drunk for *Dog Day Afternoon* (1975) and a couple of other big films. I was getting out on big projects. I did a film with Burt Reynolds, Gene Hackman and Liza Minnelli called *Lucky Lady* (1974), which was down in Mexico. The three biggest stars in the world at the time. All of them. This is way back in 1974; they were all making a million dollars, which was unheard of then. I had a nice little part in that movie. I was two weeks in Mexico. I spent that two weeks absolutely blitzed out of my mind drunk. So, you do that, you pay your dues for it and Hollywood is a very, very small town. So, that reputation spread. You know, if you're a star and you're a drunk, if you're Richard Burton, that's one thing, but I'm an unproven actor so the phone quits ringing. And I think this was really because I did some TV movies and I had a pretty good resume, but I wasn't killing anybody and I wasn't getting leads.

I was so desperate back in the day when I sobered up and stopped drinking; I said, "I'm going to get work." I used to do these scenes for casting directors. I did a couple of them a week. I did them fifty-two weeks, twice a week for a whole year. I did a hundred and four of them. I got exactly two one-day gigs from it. It was incredible that the money I made from those two days paid for the entire acting break. It was almost to the penny and I thought that's not a way to get a job in this town. But that was back in the days where you could get on the lot or sneak on the lot and I was recognized a little bit at Universal, Paramount, and such and could get on the lot. You could get the breakdown so you could take a look at what was being cast and I would dress as that character. I would go into that casting office dressed as that character and, I mean, I was a madman and I embarrassed these casting directors. But then a couple of them called me in the next week as a madman, as a lunatic. I did *Apocalypse Now* (1979) for three months.

How did you get on *Apocalypse Now*?

I was actually doing a movie with Telly Savalas and my brother, you know, had the lead as "Willard" in *Apocalypse Now*. My brother had a heart attack on the set and we all knew he was in a hospital in Manila and he was stable and he was going to live, but then I got a telephone call I think from Paramount or something to come on down and have my picture taken and do a little audition with my shirt off. So I said, "Oh, okay." I went down there and it's like within three days I had to get out of this contract with Telly Savalas. A beautiful guy. This was after his series. In this particular movie, he was playing a doctor and I was one of the mental patients. But, a sweet, sweet man. We were at a juncture where I was shot in the picture in the hospital so they could lose me. But if I went into the ward, if I shot the next day, then they would have to keep me for the rest of the picture. It was a pretty good gig. So, I explained this all to my agent and my agent explained it all to the people there in the Philippines. The Philippines people talked to Telly Savalas and he let me go. I mean, he let me go, which meant he's gonna have to do some rewriting on the script and everything. So I got to go, but because I kind of had that ace in the hole that I already had a job and that I was an actor. I said, "The only way I'm going to the Philippines, I'm not going to go there as an understudy or a stand-in. I go there as an actor and I want an actor's contract. Otherwise, I already got a job as an actor."

What was their answer to your ultimatum?

They said sure. It seemed like a matter of hours and I asked for a script for *Apocalypse Now* and an A.D. or a P.A. came over with *Heart of Darkness*, the book. So I'm reading that on the plane. And, of course, I get to the Philippines and I'm blitzed. I'm lit like a Christmas tree and I'm afraid to introduce myself to Francis Coppola. It was an opportunity few actors have in a lifetime and there I had it and I was pissing it away. I worked with some big, big names, you know: Fred Forrest, Larry Fishburne—great, great cast. So I'm just showing to the movie world that I'm a drunk. If you look closely at *Apocalypse Now*, you can recognize me. There's some shots in there.

Aside from your voice-over work, you can be seen in the film as well?

Yes. In fact, once, when my car was stolen, I was down at the Rampart division giving an interview about the car, the description and all that, and a policeman comes down and looks at me and says, "You were in *Apocalypse Now*." And I said, "No, you're thinking of my brother." He said, "No, I know who your brother is but you were in *Apocalypse Now*." And I said, "Wow, I was. Yeah, how do you know that?" My brother had cut himself earlier with a bayonet on his chin so wherever they were in the film, they would make it look bigger. But with me, the makeup artist totally forgot to put that on my face. So, that's how he knew I was in it. And, he found my car, too. So, he was a cool guy. He has a very perceptive eye.

So, I was over in the Philippines, I got all this money. You know, it was then I think you got fifty dollars a day per diem. Plus, my salary just went back to the States. And, you know, I was getting

Joe talks with *Iron Soldier* director Brett Kelly. Shot by Steve Thompson, © Brett Kelly.

whole cities drunk. So they just kind of brought me out when they needed me to stand in someplace. And on his sets, Francis Coppola's, he had an Italian chef. Of course, there were Italian lunches and it's a big deal. He'd put out the wines, the great Italian wines and such. Well, I'd drink that then I'd take a bottle back. By the end of the day, I was blitzed. It was a great opportunity for me that I just literally pissed away.

I've been sober now for thirty-some years and there's an old adage that the best day I had drunk is worse than the worst day I had sober. That's garbage. I had some great days drunk. I had a marvelous drunk. The Philippines, three months. It was more than three months, incredible drunk. And I'd hate to say I loved every minute of it, but I did. And I think I was even drunk at the airport going back to the United States. So for me, it was a great experience. Then I sobered up.

Tell us about your experience doing voice-over work for the film.

My brother and Francis, I called him Francis, had a little falling out. That's the story I got. Martin was in Mexico anyway doing a movie. So I am in California and I am a full-blown drunk by now. I had had my license taken away. So I was out on a bike drunk. Ever ride on a bike drunk? It is not easy, man. I was literally passing by this construction site on my bike drunk and there is a forklift coming out with two pallets of bricks on it. A ton of bricks. Because he had them arranged where he didn't see me, he hit me. I'd like to think God hit me with a ton of bricks. God had a sense of humor. So I went up over the handlebars, came down, broke my collarbone. So, I can't do my bike anymore. All I can do now is drink. When you drink constantly over a long period of time, you become pickled. Your skin becomes pickled and you smell bad. You smell bad, all the time. You might not think that you smell bad, but you do because that stuff gets through your pores. But that's the position I was in and so I'm drinking, the phone rings and it's Coppola's assistant, producer Fred Roos. "Can you come up to San Francisco and do the voice over for *Apocalypse Now*?" I said, "Okay, I can do that."

So, of course, I get on the plane drunk, I get off the plane drunk. I get there the night before we're doing the voice-over drunk. I show up at his office only because it's eight o' clock in the morning, sober. I'm sober. I said, "Hello, Francis." He just gives me about a paragraph to do and I do it. He says, "Okay, go out and have some breakfast and I'll write some more." So I went out and I drank my breakfast and I came back. He had some more written for me and I did that. This went on through the day and I thought I was getting better about noon, you know? About three o'clock in the afternoon, I can barely stand up and there are some Vietnamese words that I just could not get my tongue around. I just could not pronounce them. Now I'm spending the day, at the time, with still one of the most powerful men in Hollywood—at the time the most powerful producer-director in the world. I'm spending the day with him. I mean, any actor worth his salt would have gotten two or three promises, right? And I, I'm pissing it away. I'm just showing the most powerful man in Hollywood I'm a useless drunk. Got some talent, but I'm a drunk. So, these words, I can't pronounce them and Francis gets up to me and he looks me in the eye and he's about a finger's length away from my face, nose to mouth and he says, "Can't you say the words, Joe? Can't you just say the fucking words?" I literally felt myself shrink. I literally felt myself shrink inside my body from the embarrassment and humiliation. I had never been so straight-on humiliated in my life. Those words spoke volumes. He was saying can't you leave booze alone enough for part of a day? You know, can't you give me that? So, something went off in my mind and...

That was the moment you decided to stop?

That was it. I drank the rest of the day, but that was it. That was it. That was the last day I drank.

What were you saying to yourself in your mind after that?

I had already pissed one marriage away; I was ruining a relationship on the second one. It was to me anything and everything I ever wanted to be was be an actor and I saw that just be thrown to the wind. Now, in my own defense, I grew up in a drinking culture. I had eight brothers and all of them were great, incredible drunks. I had a brother down at the local bar who would say the bishop's high, holy mass, with a sheet and it was beautiful, marvelous theatre. And I would see, because it was my brothers and because they were all actors and performers and I wanted to be like that. They were drunk and I wanted to be a drunk like them. And I succeeded. And I thought I did some great performances drunk.

What is it you feel drives creative types to drugs and alcohol?

When I was in Houston, I'm coming out of the elevator to the hotel and across from me, there's a guy lying on the floor of the elevator and he's either had a heart attack or heat stroke. Both very serious stuff. This guy I was in the elevator with, who by happenstance was an Irishman, also had medical treatment. So he went over and tended to the fellow. I was gawking at him. We all have that gawkiness in us. You know, you want to draw a crowd, have a car wreck or a fight. And I don't encourage that in myself. So, I walked away and I cried. I cried for this guy. I was going out to jog and tears were pouring out my face for this man, his problem. And I liked that about myself. I liked that I had this compassion for my fellow human beings. That I could see one in danger or in turmoil and I had that compassion for him. I think those are the tools that help me be an actor. And my wife is the same way. We feel so deeply for the people we pass on the street that are homeless.

I think that as artists maybe we want to dim that a little bit. That you see so much pain and grief and suffering in the world and you want to turn yourself off from it a little bit. Do a little dance, smoke a cigarette, and listen to some rock 'n' roll. Take yourself out of this because I'm just crying thinking about this guy. And I'm an emotional guy. I'm a very emotional guy. Now, I'm adult enough that I celebrate it. I celebrate that emotion. People see me crying, "Fuck you. That's your problem. It's not mine. I'm gonna cry until I'm all cried out about this unfortunate individual." But, then, I don't know, to be that vulnerable all the time is tough for me. So, I think that was one of the reasons for my drinking and another reason was it felt so damn good. It felt good to get drunk. I was a chick magnet when I was drunk. I always got laid when I was drunk. I was great with the women. It's like Ike Turner said when they asked him why he does drugs and he says, "Because it makes me feel good. What else do you think I do it for?" It made me feel good, but for everything you do in this life there's a price. There's a payoff. And either it's a negative payoff or it's a positive payoff. With the drinking it was just a thing of diminishing returns. I think I have a very strong belief in God, and I've been touched a number of times. They say in AA, and I'm not an AA fan, but I think if you quit drinking out of fear, you're gonna go back to it. You have to grow out of it into love. Leave it behind and move on. God bless the AA if it's keeping you from drinking. It's not my path.

Were you ever a member of AA?

Never. I went to an AA meeting and I don't want to trash AA to people who are reading this or whatever. It works. It wouldn't be out there if it didn't work. But I went to an AA meeting and I see

Joe in *Rollergator*.
Courtesy of Scott Shaw.

these guys with a cup of coffee, smoking cigarette after cigarette, and telling drunk stories. To me, they were sober drunks. I went running out of that place for a drink. I said, "If that's going to happen to me, I'm gonna go out in a blaze of glory, man. I'm not gonna waste away, you know?" I got a friend whose life is in a lot of trouble. I just talked to him yesterday. Just like me, we started drinking at the same age, came up in an alcoholic type of world. He goes to an AA meeting every day. Every day. Got his 25-year chip. Once you're done with that beast you move on. You don't have to keep conquering that beast every day. And I was blessed that I knew when I was done with drinking, I was done with drinking. We can move on now.

It's a psychological thing in nature that we as human beings, we fear things. It takes courage to overcome these fears. Some of these people at these AA meetings fear drinking. And they fear it so much. Now the human heart wants to conquer fears. Whether it's alcohol or something else. It says I'm gonna conquer that fear. I'm gonna have a drink. Now I celebrate life so much I don't need a drink. I had a show once called *Hollywood Joe*. I was out and talking to the cameraman and he had been sober for two years. He was a friend of Bill's. A friend of Bill's is what they call the guys who are alcoholics in AA. I said, "Wow, you really want it? I forget what it tastes like." And he said, "That's the problem. I don't." I think it's the same thing as when I closed that door in Dayton, Ohio, and I couldn't go back to the factory. I committed myself to being an actor. When I closed that door to booze, something happened as an actor. Something happens. You move on from it. You get a power from that. You get a grace from that. You move further. It doesn't mean if you had a terrible accident and you healed from that accident that you have to go back to the scene of that accident every day. You move on. You learn what you could from that and you're a new person now. You're a person without booze. You've got a lot to learn about the world and how it is sober.

How did you quit on your own?

I just didn't do it anymore. And now, I enjoy the company of drinkers. I do. My wife now and then has a drink and I try to let her have one too many because she celebrates and it's fun. Drinking's fun. These people, it's okay because they can control it and that's all right because that's what booze is meant for. It's meant as a gift to humanity. Jesus Christ himself drank wine and relaxed. It's a gift to humanity. I abused that gift. So it was taken from me. Those people that aren't abusing it, it's okay. They can have it. After I sobered up, I think Francis Coppola was doing a movie and it may well have been *The Cotton Club* (1984). And this was during my madman period where I was just breaking into offices. And I got the word that Francis Coppola was on the lot. I think it was Warner Brothers. I said, "I've gotta go down to see him." So I figured if I get in the gate, that's a sign. And if I find out where he's at, that's a sign. And if I get to him, I get to him. It was a lot of road blocks that can happen on that way. I got into the lot, fine. They told me where he's at, fine. So I'm thinking is it locked or so I'm thinking I'm coming around the corner from the soundstage and I'm fortifying myself to talk to Francis and I said I need a sign. Is this the right thing to do? Because I'm a madman. I'm a madman actor. I just want to work, you know? I'm gonna work.

What did the signs point to?

There was a shaft of light. Like God himself had sent the light. The soundstage door was completely open. As I turn the corner I see Francis right in the middle of the soundstage. Right in the middle of it with this little table. He's on one side, Francis facing me and somebody's talking to him. Here I go, man. I'm walking over to talk to Francis. Over to my left, it's like down in the west Texas town of El Paso where they come shooting at him where he's gotta get to his love. So there's Francis and he's in the middle of the soundstage. As I walk in the door, it's completely open. The soundstage, it's like a freeway across. They bring in the big trucks and everything, too. Fred Roos is over to my left. But unless it was incredibly obvious and he ran at a fast pace, he couldn't intercept me. So, you know I was gonna get to Francis before he did. So I saw him moving, I caught him out of the corner of my eye. I was on a mission. So, I got to Francis and I said, "Francis, Mr. Coppola, I hope you remember me."

And the actor that he was talking to turned around and it was James Farentino. A marvelous actor from the '70s and '80s. I met him on *The Final Countdown* (1980). And just a great, an Italian guy. Great guy. Anyway, so they'd let me join them there and I chatted for about 20 minutes and it was very nice. I didn't know that many name actors and it just happened that it was Jimmy so it was a very nice thing. Now, I didn't get cast in *The Cotton Club* but oddly enough, Francis' son called me and there was a movie he was doing called *Smash, Crash and Burn* about rock musicians. And he asked me if I would play the manager. So I often wondered how that came down the pike, but I think it may have come of that. But, you know, I had committed a lot of sins. Not sins, I had hurt myself professionally in this town. And I paid the dues for it. And there were casting directors that wouldn't trust me. Word as a drunk spreads fast. So I had to repair my reputation as much as I possibly could.

I'm just jumping forward a little here but Bobby Z'Dar, Linda Blair, Chuck Williams, and I did a movie in the Philippines called *Double Blast* (1994). It was a pretty good movie. So, I was over there and I was sober and I was surrounded by all this poverty and I started jogging. And I still jog to this day. And I would leave the hotel room with monies in my pocket and I would give it to the kids. Back then I was a fast jogger, so I would give it to them and then I would jog and they couldn't keep up with me. Otherwise, if I would have just given it to them I would have been mobbed and so I made kind of a practice of that every day. But the incredible poverty in the Philippines and the children...There's a garbage dump over there that was continuously on fire. And families live on this garbage dump. They live on this garbage dump and they eat the garbage from the garbage dump. Families live in the side, like mud huts built into the sides. There's so many people. There's so little room. Even middle-class people live in shacks. There's nothing there. You can't save a whole country. So, I was constantly sad there because I'm a bleeding heart in Manila and going out, seeing the poverty every day. And about six months later, from the same producer, I got an offer to go back to the Philippines. And I couldn't do it. I just said thanks, but no thanks. I've worked in twelve different foreign countries and the Philippines is far and away the poorest of them all. These people had nothing. Nothing. They subsist on garbage.

Why we as human beings can let our fellow human beings suffer like that is beyond me. During *Apocalypse Now* the Marcos regime was in power and the United States would not let Coppola use their military equipment. You got *The Final Countdown* and Kirk Douglas, they'd give him an aircraft carrier, they gave him the Nimitz. They wouldn't give Coppola an M1 rifle. Marcos gave them everything. They were real chummy with Marcos and the wife, but you could do anything you wanted to in that nation as long as you didn't talk against the government. Even when Bobby, Linda Blair, and I were over there shooting this film, even then you didn't talk against the government. That was just something you did not do. And you find that in a lot of Burma, where my friend James Chean who did *Silent Scream* (1999) is from. They got that heroine, that woman over there has just been released from house arrest. She did nothing except speak up for human rights.

Double Blast. There was a white guy who was the world's best kickboxer. He was a super kickboxer. So he was the romantic male lead and Linda was the female romantic lead and Bobby and I were the bad guys who kidnap Linda. It was a fun movie, though. If you ever can rent it it's really a fun movie. I tell you, I think Bobby Z'Dar is one of the most underrated actors in the country. And I think it's because of that big face that he has. And that people hire him because of that face. We just finished a movie called *Little Creeps* (2012) and he adopted this character. He was a college professor.

INTERVIEW WITH JOE ESTEVEZ

So, he made him this British tweed, high smoking professor. He was absolutely brilliant. I mean, he was brilliant. He stole the damn movie.

Did the narration you did for *Apocalypse Now* end up in the film? If so, how much?

My understanding now is that it is part mine and part my brother's. An interesting sidebar on that: it was St. Patrick's Day of last year on *Jeopardy* and there's a question and it said, "When the star wasn't available Joe Estevez stepped in and did the voiceover narration for what film?" And the guy got it right! "Apocalypse Now." So, hey, it's on *Jeopardy* so it must be my voice. Frankly, there's two other films at least that I've done his voice...not his whole thing, but they needed pick-ups and he wasn't available. I can now tell us apart, but for years I couldn't tell our voices apart. He's got this dental work now. In my opinion, his voice isn't as smooth as it once was. I think it was better when he was younger than it is now. That's just my opinion, though. It's interesting, I'm going to Morgan Hill here to go to the Jasper Film Festival and they're playing *Apocalypse Now*. They invited me up to comment on the movie and working on the movie and the voiceover. So I don't know, that voiceover is getting a life of its own.

How accurate was the documentary *Hearts of Darkness* (1991)?

It was bullshit. Please, she's shooting a documentary on 35mm film. You think Francis is going to let anything go without his final approval? A lot of these film people are born with a spoon in their mouth. They don't really know what it's really like to have it tough. You know, people like Chris Watson know what it's like to have it tough. To come in on the bottom rung of this film business and tough it out. A lot of people, they just assume that they're having it tough. They're not. It's smoke and mirrors in that documentary— utter nonsense.

What are your thoughts on the American Film Market as an actor?

You could go in there and it was a seller's market. They would buy anything. You would go there in the '80s and you would just show up and pick up a couple of gigs. "Hey, Joe Estevez! Listen, I've got a script if you're available." That was the good ole days. Now I go down there to see some old friends. Or if a filmmaker invites me down to sit at his booth or meet the buyers as they come in. That whole atmosphere has really changed there with the advent of the Internet and selling films in packaging deals to Netflix, etc. The market is quickly becoming obsolete. I think it's a dead horse. They just don't realize it's dead yet. I still go down there. It's kind of nice for my ego to meet some people. People still ask me if I'm available, but the difference now is the films never get off the ground. It's seen its good days, but is on the way out now.

What movies have you been in that you view as underrated?

Murder-in-Law (1989). I think it's a terrific movie. I'd have to call it a black comedy. It was just terrific. Everyone in it was absolutely at the top of the game. Actors were terrific, script was terrific. It was in the genre; if you had to put it in a genre, it would be a horror genre. I guess there weren't enough killings. The killings there weren't gruesome enough. It was plot-driven rather than killer-driven. There wasn't a killing every seven pages of the script. Such a great title, too. Those in charge for some reason changed the title. I don't even know what it's called now. That movie should've done a whole lot better than it did. I did a movie called *Jumping for Joy* (2002). Terrific movie. I mean, just a terrific movie. I play a former basketball coach of the Utah Jazz named Frank Layton. It's about this young lady who plays on a varsity basketball team. I don't know what really happened, but the movie never got any kind of release. It's always about a money thing. They feel like they're not getting paid enough for the movie or they can't find the proper distributor. I think those two are underrated. I'm proud of my performances in them, too. Both characters I played are very subtle. A lot of movies I might eat a lot of scenery and such, but these two are very subtle. They are quiet characters, contained inside of themselves. I'm proud of them both. Conrad Brooks introduced me to a fellow named James Chean. James brought me in for a movie called *Silent*

Scream. It was Dana Plato's last film. It's a horror film also, but very much in the style of Hitchcock. Marvelous film. I don't know if anyone else enjoyed being in it, but I enjoyed the hell out of myself. The film kind of just died. It's just never got out there and it should've got out there. It just never saw the light of day. I think with filmmakers...it's a shame...but like, with yourself, you're a filmmaker, but you also have the ability to be business savvy. A lot of filmmakers don't have that business savvy. Good filmmakers. They make a good, good film. In trying to get it out there, for the public to see, they have no idea. Usually they end up giving it away to some schlock quote distributor who sells it as a piece of meat to anybody who'll give them a few bucks. They probably never even watch the damn thing. The filmmaker never sees a penny. That's the way it goes 90% of the time. That's a shame. A lot of good films aren't seen. A lot of good actors don't get in the public eye like they should. Another one is *Cordoba Nights* (2007). I play a mob guy in it. Quirky, quirky film. I'm proud of it. I like that film.

Tell me about meeting Donald G. Jackson for the first time.

It was akin to going up the river and meeting Captain Kurtz, I tell you, only more dramatic. The first movie I did for him, there's all these candles lit and then there's Donald sitting there cross-legged Buddha style in kind of a Zen meditation. "Hey, Don, Joe Estevez here, nice to meet you." "Joe Estevez...an honor, sir." He was a character. The mystique of Donald Jackson is that of the Ed Wood's. You heard so much about him—his reputation preceded him. He didn't let me down. He was everything I expected him to be. The first thing that he did after shooting that movie and kind of explaining what he was doing was he paid me. He paid well. I thought, "Wow, that's cool." You always have to respect the film-maker that pays in cash. You get that upfront. You don't have to worry about him getting lost. He wasn't one of those you have to chase around for the money. I liked that about Don.

I showed a friend *The Roller Blade Seven* and I think his jaw was down the entire time. He just kept repeating that it was "genius."

***Guns of El
Chupacabra.***
Courtesy of
Scott Shaw.

What's really surprising with Don is that you do one movie for
him and he'd cut you up and mix you into four different movies. You
don't know you're starring in all these other movies. There's nothing I
can do with it. They can make a marvelous tongue-in-cheek film
like *Zombiegeddon* (2003) and people are stealing it, cutting parts
out of it and whatever. I think it's a compliment in a way. What you
do is worthy of being stolen. If they can make a couple of bucks,
what the hell? I got paid for it. I'm ok with it.

**You worked with porn star Jill Kelly in several of Jackson's films.
What are your thoughts on porn stars acting in mainstream
films?**

I would much rather they act in mainstream films than pornography.
I think that's not good for their souls. I don't mind working with
them at all. They're human beings. I find they're very vulnerable.
Sometimes it's tough to get them out of their shell, but it's very easy
to get beyond that. You talk to them and they have this persona
they put out. Yet, they're very vulnerable. I think that's how they
were caught up in the pornography in the first place. We have so
much to offer. To say, "This is my body..." They shouldn't do it,
but there shouldn't be a market out there...we're such an insensitive
and vile society that we make money off this. There's much more
shame on the producers and directors than on the actors who are

more victims. That's how I feel about these people. We're all actors, we're just vulnerable. I treat them very gently. As they do me. We show our emotions, what we are going out on the set.

What are your thoughts on Jackson and Scott Shaw's Zen Style of filmmaking?

I have worked for about four years for a company called "Die Laughing" which was a murder mystery company. We got a lot of press on this. I always liked improvisation. With this murder mystery stuff it would be totally improvisation. We would go for three days from Friday night to Sunday afternoon with this comedy mystery. It would be a skeleton script and we would just fill in everything. Working with professional actors, really great professional actors. I got very, very comfortable with myself and improvisation. I got very relaxed. I relied on myself that if I relaxed that whatever gag or what I wanted to do would come to me. So when I worked with Donald Jackson, "We don't need no stinkin' script," I was absolutely fine with that. I've got a script, I try to change the hell out of it, you know? I'd try to change Shakespeare if I could. It was fine with me. I love that kind of filmmaking. Sometimes, it would be a dud, but other times you try something and some incredible magic would happen. Don never judged. He never said that was bad or that was good. I liked it a lot.

Did that help you when you were doing the scene with William Smith in Zombiegeddon?

Oh, yes. Absolutely. Bill never had time to study his lines or whatever. He'd memorize his first line and then it was gone. I kind of had my lines. So I improvised what he was supposed to say to me and then I answered it. Yes, it did. I wouldn't have had the gall to try that if I hadn't.

You actually seemed really comfortable, almost as if you were more comfortable doing improv than a script. With you being the puppeteer of the scene, it also ended up being the scene people talk about the most from the movie. They always mention

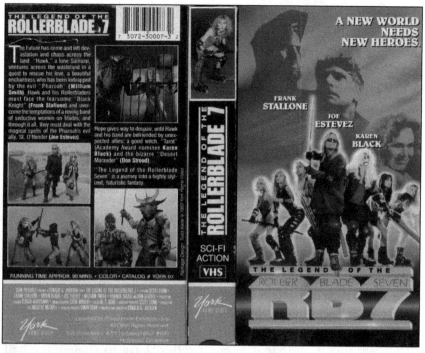

Legend of the Roller Blade Seven. Courtesy of Scott Shaw.

there's certain movements you make that were highlights to them.

I thought that was the director that told me to make those movements. Acting is just reacting. I'm just reacting. Sometimes you get it right. Sometimes you get it not so right. What the heck. First of all, I loved that outfit Bill was wearing. That was marvelously over the top. Looking at him is hard as hell. This acclaimed actor, winner of all these awards—God bless William Smith for coming out there to do it. He's an established actor. He's a big star to be willing to make himself look silly.

What advice would you give to a director in regard to working with actors?

Let them act. You cast them because you felt that they could do the part. Let them create. Don't block the scene for them. Let them block the scene themselves. Let their own energy take them where

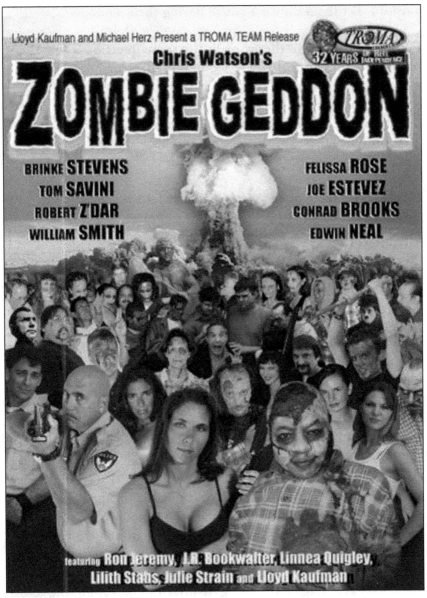

Lloyd Kaufman and Michael Herz Present a TROMA TEAM Release

Chris Watson's

TROMA

32 YEARS OF HELL BENT INDEPENDENCE

ZOMBIE GEDDON

BRINKE **STEVENS**
TOM **SAVINI**
ROBERT **Z'DAR**
WILLIAM **SMITH**

FELISSA **ROSE**
JOE **ESTEVEZ**
CONRAD **BROOKS**
EDWIN **NEAL**

featuring **Ron Jeremy, J.R. Bookwalter, Linnea Quigley, Lilith Stabs, Julie Strain** and **Lloyd Kaufman**

Zombiegeddon **DVD cover.**

they want to go in the scene. That's the way it used to be, old school. Then set your lights according to where the actors take it. Have confidence in your actors. If you loosen up and let them go they can show you dimensions and nuances in the scene that you never thought were there. Let go of the reins. Actors are actors for a reason. Let them do what you're paying them to do.

I'm going to change the word in the same question a few times here. How do you feel you're viewed by directors?

Some of them are a little afraid of me. Most of them are glad to have me on board. They trust me. After they've worked with me 10 or 15 minutes they feel pretty comfortable with me. I put them at ease.

How do you feel you're viewed by your fellow actors?

I think most of the time okay. I don't mean to be, but sometimes I just have instincts about a scene. I try to direct the fellow actors into this way of playing the scene. You know, instead of letting us all work together and develop it. Sometimes I'm a little heavy handed. There are other actors like that. When I meet other actors like that I just stand up for myself. If I agree with them, I'll do it, but if I don't I'll say, "That's nice. That's not the way I see it. I see it being this way so let's see if we can come together on this." I think most of my fellow actors like me. I like most of my fellow actors. We're all very vulnerable people. When you're acting, you trust another actor with your emotions, passions, love, and all your fears. You trust your fellow actor with that. It makes them trust you. There's always the bad apple in the bunch. I did a movie called *Cake: A Wedding Story* (2007). Will Wallace was directing, great movie. It's about a wedding and I'm the father of the bride. I play a clumsy, bashful, inept kind of person. It's not a particularly easy kind of character to be that vulnerable in front of a camera. I thought I did a pretty damn good job with it. I was very much a klutz and the brunt of the jokes. To play that kind of character, it's not as easy as a tough guy, but I gave myself to it. Most of the actors out there respect that you went there and did it. I'm at Ralph's Market after the movie has wrapped and this one guy who was the tough guy asshole in the movie comes down the aisle, "Hey, sissypants!" I'm just doing my shopping. I'm just Joe Estevez now. "Hey, sissypants!" Instead of saying, "Hey, Joe, how you doing, man? Long time no see." I said, "Hey, fuck you. Fuck you. Who in the fuck do you think you're talking to?" That was pretty much the end of that conversation. It was a little surprise that I was that way, but they got to know that doesn't play when I'm out there in real life. I could understand it from a grip or a citizen that's seen the movie, but from a fellow actor? Unforgiveable. Totally unforgiveable.

I've worked with a lot of actors that haven't acted that much. And I've worked with a lot of professionals. Once the director calls, "Action," we're all created equal. We're all in that same boat. It's what you bring to that scene, no matter how long you've been doing this, is the measure of your talent. I love actors, I really do. A lot of places I go, like Chicago, Salt Lake City, and Florida, I give talks to the local actors. I don't teach acting because it's something you can't teach, but I try to inspire these kids. I try to be an inspiration and a comfort. I tell them that acting is great fun. It's a marvelous life. If you choose to do it, welcome aboard. It's good to have you here. Actors are good people. I think in Hollywood the climate has changed. They come to Hollywood and have no concept of what an actor really is. I don't understand these people. They're so shallow and misguided. How did they get to this age with being so misinformed about what life is really about? Hollywood is where all the bad men and crazies come to. They're lined up and down Hollywood Boulevard. They fill all the coffee shops. These people aren't actors. They're pretenders. They have nothing to do with acting. They have something in their personality that they need to be seen. I would be an actor if there was no such thing as film. I wrote two plays. I just did a read-through with Ed Asner. We have a paid staged reading August 29. I love that. That's spontaneity. It's the real essence of acting. If I could work just on stage, that would be absolutely fine with me. I don't like all the waiting with film. The main word is acting. To act. I think a lot of these kids come out here and they have never done a stage play in their life. They never want to do a stage play. They just want to get in front of a camera and write back home to tell them, "Hey, I'm in a movie."

How do you feel you are viewed by fans?

I think that anybody who understands independent films, and doesn't cast them off because they don't have the greatest sets—I

Courtesy of
Dr. Scott Shaw.

think they regard me pretty good. There are people who watch movies and just cast them out because it's not a mainstream film. They say, "Anybody in that film must be off too," because they just don't understand. I forgive them for that. There's nothing that I can do about that. I work so steady that I must have some fan base out there that appreciates what I'm doing. I appreciate those people.

On this same topic, you've done a few conventions.

I usually don't do them. First of all, I have this fear that if I go to a convention no one's going to recognize me. In the few that I've done, I give away my pictures. I don't sell them. I don't think anything about it except I feel uncomfortable selling my picture. I think that somebody who would honor me by wanting my picture, I'll give it away. This guy came up to me the other day and said he went in this restaurant in backwater Texas and asked for directions and there was my picture on the wall. I thought, "Oh, shit, isn't that cool?" I'm sure that guy did not have to pay for that picture or that picture wouldn't be up there at all. The conventions are great for fans of horror to meet the stars that they see in the pictures, and that's cool. I've got no problem with it in general. For me personally, I feel a little uncomfortable with it, but that's just me. Having said that, a guy called me and wants to put Bobby Z'Dar and me up for the Chiller convention. A 2-for-1 deal. I'll do that because I love Bobby so much. I would sit there with Bobby and do that Chiller thing. That would be the only exception.

How do you feel about tabloid journalists?

They're bastards. What a bunch of scumbags. There's an old adage about the stars having an ego, some sort of sick relationship with themselves that one feeds off the other. There's no such thing as bad press if your name is mentioned. I think it's just disgusting. Things that are just out and out freaking lies. There was stuff said about me in conjunction with *Two and a Half Men*, me wanting to take over that show—just garbage. You have absolutely no defense. There's this lawsuit where this guy's suing Charlie because I couldn't do a reality show. I've never in my life wanted to do a reality show. Just ludicrous stuff that they get a-hold of. They just throw it out there for the gullible, brainless masses. It's a necessary evil, but I could do no deal without it. I think they are part of what is wrong with this country. They have no soul and character. They do, but they don't realize they do. I think in this life, for everything you do, you pay the price. One way or another, sooner or later, you pay the price for your actions.

How do you feel you are viewed by critics?

It depends on the movie. It's funny; you take *Soultaker* (1990) for instance. When Soultaker first came out, I got rave reviews. There wasn't a bad review in the bunch. Great reviews all the way around. The film itself got great reviews. All the actors got great reviews. When it went on *Mystery Science Theater 3000*, they cut the piss out of it. Once it got to *Mystery Science Theater 3000*, it was put out there like, "Look at this joke!" So the audience said, "Oh, yeah, this is a piece of shit." I think people in general are lemmings; they're led around by the nose. I think if critics say this is good, they go, "Oh, yeah, that's good." If critics say it's a piece of shit, they go, "Oh, yeah, this is a piece of shit." I'm doing this play now about this guy who is in a holding cell they have for before they go into the chamber to be executed. He's an actor. His crime was that he killed the critics. All the actors love him and everything; he's such a big hero. Instead of like the news reporters covering the death, it's all critics. They're reviewing how he's going to die. It's just a one act. Hopefully, it'll be a fun play. Critics are just one opinion. They write to try to be cute. To try to make themselves look good. Often times it's at the movie's expense. I think the critics are oftentimes bought off and paid for. I don't mean directly like, "Here's $10,000." I mean trips to Vegas. They understand they're supposed to lean toward a good review. There are a lot of critics out there who have their own personal vendettas. They have actors they dislike. If you're one that they dislike then you're in trouble. I don't give a shit if you're Marlon Brando, there's people out there that don't like you. I don't care if you're the worst actor in the world, there's people out there that like you. I think all critics are just frustrated actors.

You worked with little people in *Little Creeps* (2012).

Accent on creeps.

What are your thoughts on little people actors?

We've discussed this at length. It's kind of like working with animals. I don't like them. It's just an ego thing. You can be doing the most brilliant scene that you have ever done in your life and if you're sharing that scene with the little people then you are invisible. Totally invisible. The audience says, "Oh, look at the cute little…oh, he's picking his ass. Oh, isn't that something?" Moviemakers and producers are abusing and using them just because they are little people. Having said that, there are some little people who are terrific actors. Peter Dinklage is phenomenal. It's tough enough to be a little person, but to be taken seriously as an actor—God bless him, this guy is terrific. He deserves everything that he got and more. It's a tough life they have, but I'd rather they be in someone else's scene. However, I don't want them to be overlooked.

Give me some examples of work you've turned down. What are some reasons you've turned down work?

I have turned down stuff lately. My reasons are that I'm feeling myself much closer to my leaving this planet, much closer to answering for the things that I do. That's one reason. The other reason is that I've become much more conscious of what is good

Toad Warrior.
Courtesy of
Scott Shaw.

and what isn't. I realized how much movies influence people. I don't want to put that kind of energy out there. This one filmmaker has a big-time producer. I read the part he wanted me to play and I have to tell him, "I can't do this. I don't want to put this out there. I don't want to put that kind of vulgarity out there." The money I make on a movie I spend it, but I only have one soul, you know? I've only got one person I get up and see in the mirror. I've got to live with that. I did a movie in Australia. I said, "Sure, I'll take it." I didn't read the script. I didn't realize the movie was about violence. Just violence. It was one of those torture films. I wasn't being tortured. My character was actually a redeeming character. I will never, ever do a film like that again. It's just vulgar. It's pornography of violence. I don't care if you're a schmuck of a filmmaker or big-time filmmaker. Just the pornography of violence has no redeeming quality. I mean that in a moral sense. That's garbage. These big-time filmmakers are putting this stuff out to mass audiences. These audiences eat it up. Shame on them. They have this brilliant talent and that's what they use it for. They've sold their souls. They sold out. They have the big cars, big mansions, and the jewels...they're shallow people. I've lost my way now and then, but I usually find my way back to the main road. I try to stay on the main road. When I get off the main road, I know that I've gotten off the main road.

Are there any other movies that come to mind that you wish you hadn't done because of content?

Well, *Beach Babes From Beyond* (1993). There's two versions of it. One's filled with soft porn that is totally out of context that the filmmaker put in after we finished. It wasn't in the original script. There's some other names beside myself that are in there—that's not the film that we agreed to do. Burt Ward was in it. He had a name and there's couple others. Stallone's mother was in it. Don Swayze was in it. And Don Swayze's a helluva actor. None of us saw that coming. It was a great concept. These three women come from Mars. There's some stuff with bare-breasted ladies and I thought, "That's not going to hurt anybody, what the hell?" I'm human. I have to pay my rent. I have to pay that child support. I have to take care of my children. I have to take care of myself. Now, I read the script. Like most actors, I used to just go to my part. Then I'd tell the guy, "Yeah, I'll take it." I've paid the price a number of times for not reading the script. Even if they ask me to do two scenes or something, I'll read the whole script now. I have to be more responsible for myself now.

Did they make it seem like it would be more like a beach type of movie? A throwback?

Exactly.

And then they just slipped soft porn in and...

Exactly. And if you look at that movie it's totally incongruous to the plot. It's just a simple Frankie Avalon, Annette Funicello go to the beach type of thing. Don and myself, we were kind of making a name for ourselves and we were doing some nicer roles. When this came out, we kind of became ones who were exploiting our last names, kind of jokes, and taking the money. So it didn't help me at all.

Have you spoken to the director of *Beach Babes From Beyond* since?

No, I don't even know who the hell he is. I wouldn't recognize him if I saw him on the street. I wouldn't recognize the name if someone told me. I may have talked to him and not known it.

The director, David Decoteau, used a pseudonym.

Did he?

Ellen Cabot.

That bastard.

He uses a pseudonym when he does soft core.

There was no pseudonym when the contract was signed.

It sounds like it was a total curveball.

Yeah, because there's two versions.

What is the version you were shown?

That whole middle part; the soft core was not in the script. I was just Uncle Bud: beach bum. Just Uncle Bud.

Yeah, it was actually a lot like Mark Harmon's character in *Summer School* (1987).

Not that I'm that careful, but once it's in the editing room, it's pretty much out of your control. What's an actor going to do? Is he going to sue these people? You can't find the people at the company in the first place. And if you did, it would take thousands and thousands of dollars. So, when it gets in the editing room, it's out of your control. So that's that on the very sore subject of *Beach Babes From Beyond*.

How many movies have you done with Frank Stallone?

Probably four that I absolutely know of. There's probably more that we're in, but never saw each other.
  The Garbage Man (1996), it's fun. It's a fun movie. It's a comedy. And Frank's a helluva rock 'n' roller—guitar man and all that. And

they got a sister, Silvi or something with an "s." What a doll. I did a movie with her husband. What a lovely, beautiful lady. She's like mother earth. Just the Italian mother. Only, she was slim and beautiful. I really, really enjoyed her. And I did a movie with Sly's mom, *Beach Babes From Beyond*, which I don't like to talk about too much. I've worked with everybody, but Sly, in that family.

You've worked with Don Swayze, Joey Travolta, Jackie Stallone, Frank Stallone, and others with famous relatives. Does conversation ever go to that topic?

It never does. I think that all of us individually and as a group, we hate that shit. We hate that stuff. Frank is a star in his own right. He's been working since before his brother. In a matter of fact, I think we go out of our way to avoid it. A lot of people don't see us as "us." I've been in over 200 movies and they say, "You're Martin Sheen's brother." I respect Frank for the artist that he is. Trying to think back, I've worked with Joey Travolta and I've worked with his sister doing voiceovers. All us producers, directors, and actors—it's like we're inside this cage. How the outside world sees us is totally different than how we perceive ourselves. When I see Frank Stallone, I don't think, "Oh, geez, can you get me Sly's autograph?" Somebody from the outside world might ask that. I see Frank Stallone and I appreciate him for the artist that he is. Chad McQueen is another one, Steve McQueen's son. Anthony Quinn's son did a movie with me in Texas. His father was such a bigger-than-life character that he told stories that his father told. It's the story that's the star, not his father. That's strange that you ask that because that never came up. I get a lot of actors that come up and say, "Hey, I worked with your brother." That's cool. I don't usually take the conversation any further. I think that's about it, other actors tell me they worked with my brother and my nephews. As far as the Chad McQueens and Frank Stallones, they don't bring it up. I don't either.

I'm going to use Don Swayze as an example here. I know he's continued to train as an actor. I think he's a great, underrated actor. Do you think the fact that he's Patrick Swayze's brother has hurt him?

Oh yeah, it hurts us all. Absolutely. Don Swayze is a brilliant actor. He's also certifiably mad. He's either the maddest person I know or the bravest person I know. He has this adrenaline rush that he has to get a fix for, I guess, three times a day. He does the crazy things— parachute jumping, anything that involves risking your life. He crushed his foot and had to get a new prosthesis. He's still out there as crazy as ever, which I love him for. He's a terrific actor. He's very intense. Good, focused actor. Let me put this out there generally speaking. I don't know, maybe his brother has put him in some of his movies. My family has not helped me. I don't think his family has helped him. That is the way it is with a lot of siblings—a lot of sons and daughters and such. Because of that I think the business looks and thinks, "Well, if they're relative doesn't help them then they must be damaged goods." Ron Howard doesn't have a movie that Clint Howard isn't in. That's cool. I'm thrilled for Clint that his brother does that. Plus, Clint gets work on his own. Any time his brother is there and able to throw him a bone, he does. The business is going to look at that and say, "Well, Clint's cool. His brother is a big-time producer, director and he takes care of him..." I think that there's this idea that if the relative doesn't care for them then they're damaged goods. It's not something that's spoken out loud, but it's just something that's there.

How did the roles with Martin come about?

No Code of Conduct (1998) I knew the producer, even back before he was in the business. He is the guy who brought me in. They were shooting that movie in Arizona. Charlie and my brother didn't even realize I was in the movie until I showed up on the set. That's how that came about. I did a thing called *Flatland* (2007). Will Wallace, who's been very good to me, was instrumental in getting me in that. He also did *Doonby* (2012). It's coming out in a whole bunch of theaters. Will Wallace got me the part in *Flatland*. My brother had nothing to do with that. The one part that my brother had some-thing to do with, and I'm very thankful to him, was the first film I ever did, *The Story of Pretty Boy Floyd*, which he got me an audition for. I auditioned and I got the role. The very next part after that was a movie called *California Kid* (1974). I was up for the lead in that and I was so stupid. I said, "You know, you ought to get Martin Sheen to play this." They did. I played his brother. That film was in my ballpark and I told them to get Martin Sheen for that because I was just new in Hollywood. I thought leads were going to be offered to me all the time. *The Story of Pretty Boy Floyd* was the first and only time that he threw me a bone at all. There's many times I've asked him to be in my pictures and he declined. I have had some legitimate offers from producers to those guys to do pictures I'm in and they've all declined. I don't know what it is. If there were something wrong with me I think it would have surfaced by now. It's something they have to overcome. It's certainly not something I have to overcome.

What was their reaction when they did see you and what was that set like?

They pretty much ignored me. Martin was not very kind to me. I had my daughter Amanda with me. The producer invited me, my brother, and Charlie to dinner. Neither one of them showed up. I was the only one who showed up for the dinner. We never got together. Nobody came to say, "Hey, Joe, let's do some dinner or hang." It was nothing. Let me say this, though. Charlie was going through some difficult periods at the time with the things that Charlie goes through. My brother was preoccupied with that. That could have been one of the reasons why. I'm usually a pretty fun guy to be around on set and I was no different with this film. I made a lot of friends on that set that I still have to this day. I enjoyed doing the movie, I enjoyed there's something on my resume where I've worked with my family, but I think the term "cold shoulder" comes to mind.

There's another one called *Dillinger and Capone* (1995), right?

Yeah, that was Roger Corman. I forgot about *Dillinger and Capone*. The whole premise of *Dillinger and Capone* was, is that my brother was playing Dillinger. The story is it wasn't Dillinger who was killed out in front of that theatre in Chicago—it was somebody that looked like him. When Dillinger saw that, that gave him a chance to go off and make a new life. That was the premise of that movie. I worked for Corman before that. When my brother accepted that role, of course I was perfect to play the guy that did get shot in front of the theatre. My brother didn't say, "Get somebody else," but he didn't say, "Get this guy," either. That's my understanding. You know what, I don't know. Maybe he did say, "Get my brother," and I don't know it. That one I don't know about. He may have.

What is your view of micro-filmmaking?

I think it's fine if it's watchable. The talent is much more important than money. In the general scheme of things, *film noir* came about because they were less expensive films. They just didn't have the money so they created all these marvelously creative things. I love *film noir* and it came about by trying to save a few bucks. If you can tell your story, say some things pretty simply, but very profound. If you can do a movie for $100, excellent, do it for a $100. *Zombiegeddon*…whether it cost three million or 10,000 it's *Zombiegeddon*. It gets a life of its own; people appreciate it for what it is. Money becomes secondary. A lot of the films I look back on, and am most proud of, are the films I got paid less for. I see the filmmaker has some talent, some vision, and I would like to be a part of that. He's got a script and it's unique. A lot of times I don't change a word. There's a script I read that's brilliant. The writing is absolutely brilliant. When I auditioned for the film, every actor memorizes it so they give a performance and not just a reading, but I had an incredibly difficult time memorizing how this guy writes. It was just a second language to him. It was so marvelous. It was so unique the way he wrote. I memorized every word the way he wrote it. There are filmmakers out there and I'd like to work with them whether it's a micro-budget or mainstream big budget. I don't want to keep doing the same old schlock that I've done a 1,000 times. I was doing a movie over Christmas. I'm getting this blood on my face and we're setting up this scene where this gal pounds me into the steps. I said to myself and anybody that could hear me, "This is the last time I'm doing this. This is not acting." I won't do that again—I won't say won't. There are bigger paychecks than others.

Have you ever been bothered by being flown across the country and working for a small fee?

Small fees are relative. I remember I went to Manchester, England, with my wife. It was supposed to have our friend Richard Norton, but they didn't have money for Richard. They wanted both of us. I think I was there for a week and they paid me a thousand dollars. I'm in Manchester, England—this is cool. It didn't bother me at all. That's fine. You work for a living in a factory, that's a lot of money. Money's really relative. I won't do it anymore, but I've worked for big money and small money.

We had breakfast with an actor who was complaining about how low a straight-to-video director paid. The amount stated is less than you would get paid for a micro-film. What are your thoughts on someone who works regularly and usually has a decent budget paying below what you'd get on the typical micro-film?

The two movies I did with him I think were union movies. He hasn't called me and maybe that's why, because he's taking the money and adding on an extension to his house and taking what's left to make the film with it. You know, a lot of producers do that. They get a quarter million dollars and take 125 off the top and low ball everything else. It's a shame. It's a form of thievery, but it's done by some. First time you don't know any better. The investor doesn't realize it's just nonsense. I don't want to pass any judgment. I don't know how much money he gets to make these films. In my experience with him, I was paid at least union scale and maybe a little more— I don't remember what I made on that. I always thought he was a good guy to me on those two films. I really can't say.

Let's talk about *Soultaker*. You actually have a fondness for that film, correct?

Soultaker was a good film. It's a little bit outdated now. It was made in the '80s. It takes, like any good movie should, a reasonable time for the plot to unravel. It's a good, solid film. I think what they did with it on *Mystery Science Theater 3000*, they made a comedy and

Shot by Steve Thompson, © Brett Kelly.

made fun of it. Nothing I can do about that. *Soultaker* deserved the
original reviews it got. There was a [studio] film that came out and
a lot of reviewers said it [*Soultaker*] was better. They said *Soultaker*
was a more solid premise. It did very, very well. It was a top video
sale of the week. It was very good to me because it put me on the
map. I've been working ever since *Soultaker* came out. Originally,
they had asked me to play the mayor in it. I read the script and the
actual soultaker was originally scripted as some kind of faceless
monster. I got the script when it was about in its third rewrite.
The soultaker had a personality. I loved the character. I found this
marvelous melancholy in this character that I wanted to play. It
wasn't all, but "Hey, Soultaker has feelings, too!" I liked that about
him. I think the audience saw that and it kind of helped me to be
a working actor. That was the first film that I did with Bobby
Z'Dar. *Soultaker* was my first experience with Bobby Z'Dar. I was a
little bit in awe of the big fella. Especially when he's in that
costume as my boss. They did this marvelous stuff with his hair and
he had that great Kirk Douglas jaw. I was in awe of Bobby. He was
and still is a puppy dog. If I may say now, he, like all of us, has had

From the collection of Joe Estevez.

his troubles. He's turned off some producers and directors. He feels genuinely bad for that now. He's put away all the booze and whatever. Bob is very focused. He's very concerned about his art as an actor now. I'm very proud of him. You know, *Little Creeps*, Bobby is the one who suggested me for the lead. The director cast me and I got to work with Bobby again. He was absolutely marvelous. He plays a professor with this British accent, the type that smokes the pipe and spends his whole academia life behind college doors.

Bobby is absolutely brilliant with that character. I didn't appreciate how good the director of that movie was at the time. I thought Vivian's crafting of the writing of the film was a heck of a job. She got the idea of that movie from a dream. I'm very thankful that I got chosen for *Soultaker* and that it was a good movie. If you see the original movie and not that other version, I think horror aficionados will appreciate it. It comes at you from a whole different place. It scares you from someplace you didn't know you could be scared from. Like being in an earthquake. "Where did that come from?" It's kind of the same thing with *Soultaker*, except it's safer since you're watching instead of participating.

Looking back at it, are you surprised that you are identified with this film of the 200-plus you've done?

Oh, yeah. Absolutely. I've done more prominent films. I'm much more proud to be identified with *Soultaker* than some of the other films I've done. That doesn't bother me at all. I'm proud of that. I get a lot of fans that saw me in that. Because of that they've been loyal and whatever else I do they try to make a point to see it. I'm very appreciative of that.

Are there any of the films that you are embarrassed by that you'd mention?

The Catcher (2000). I think I'm a pretty good actor. I just missed the boat on that. I was doing my "Martin Sheen"—I just screamed through the thing. A few little nuances would've been in order. Let me go on the record to say I'm officially ashamed of *The Catcher*. If I walked over and looked at my filmography I could probably name four dozen offhand. There are a lot of times where the film didn't come out well, but the acting is good. Once the film is made, it's out of the actor's hands. There's a film called *Scar* (2005) that I thought would be much better. A lot of that stuff is out of my hands. I would have more nuances with my character. A lot of times you're on a set and you have to get a shot and it's getting dark. You don't have the luxury of getting the coverage or rehearsing the shot. They just set it up and shoot it. That's the nature of independent film. That's the land where I live. I play by those rules. Sometimes you play by those rules and don't get the shot that otherwise you would have gotten. The general audience out there doesn't understand that. They don't understand that you could take a wooden piece of stick and if you have enough money you can get it enough coverage, that brilliant piece of stick will be a brilliant actor. Most TV actors are good. But there are some terrible, terrible actors that are made to look good because of the editing. You sit there and look at TV and how quick those cuts are. They're not on screen for four seconds before they cut to someone else to someone else then to something else. You can't help but give a performance. When you're doing an independent film and that camera is hanging on you for two and three minutes and you've got to produce, that's a whole different story. You better bring your talents to the set. There are movies out there I could have been better in. I'm not making excuses. I'm just saying that is where I live. There's an old adage that if you do a movie that isn't up to par, you don't want it on you. If this is going to be a turkey then I at least want my performance to come out. At least they could say, "That movie sucked, but Estevez wasn't bad." Sometimes that's the best you can hope for. I realize that. I took the check. I think the audience has to look beyond certain things. Independent moviemakers just don't have the money. They can't hire a 50-piece orchestra. They can't afford adr. If you can do adr at all it's probably in somebody's closet. You can't get the best sets. Usually you're stealing the scene. You're hoping you get the scene done before the police come and chase you off. You're at the mercy of the sounds and people passing by watching you shoot. Independent films are guerilla. All the distractions going on out there, it's amazing that some of these films are as good as they are considering the obstacles they had to put up with.

Then there's *Doonby*. The last thing was just a voiceover when I'm 30 years younger. I just blew it. It was melodramatic. This movie is playing all over the country. It's going to do really well. Yesterday, the director said, "You know, Joe, I'm in town. If you're in town, let's go redo that last voiceover." I was thrilled to death. You don't often get a chance to do that. I went in and redid the adr on that voiceover and I'm completely pleased with it. *Doonby* has a budget. These other movies don't have a budget. If I miss it the first time around, you don't get a second chance. If you're working with a new director, they're afraid to tell you, "Listen, I think you can do better." They're intimidated and let a performance go that could otherwise be better. I try to ask them because when it's off, an actor knows it's off. I'll ask, "Can we do that again?" A lot of times they'll let it slide. That's a problem. As a director, you've got to speak up. You've only got that one shot.

I'm getting us off topic, but to follow up, how do you handle promoting the films that are bad? When you're at the premiere, etc.

Usually I handle it by just avoiding it. If I have to go there, I usually sit toward the back and cringe a lot. Take the paycheck, take your medicine. "You really stunk up the place!" "Yeah, I know. I'm sorry." You've got to live with it. I talk about the good things. I ignore the bad things. That's just the nature of the beast. Way back in the day I was at the VSDA in Vegas. Mom and pops owned the video stores. I was there pushing a film for David Winters. I think the film was *Armed for Action* (1992). We were having a great dinner there. Carradine was there and a lot of the B-movie stars. David Winters had invited us. I'm sitting right next to the big distributors. One of them asks me, "What'd you think of *Armed for Action*?" I said, "Well, geez, quite frankly it's not my cup of tea. I'd rather do a movie that had some substance to it." David Winters had smoke coming out of his head. After dinner, he got me aside and said, "Christ, Estevez, look. If you can't say anything good about the movie, please don't say anything at all. I'm trying to sell this damned thing." I realized what a total and complete ass I had made of myself. This guy is paying me to be there. He's buying the dinner; he's putting me up in a hotel. At this dinner, I'm dissing his movie to a big distributor that wanted to buy it. I could have handled that same thing by saying, "You know, I really enjoyed my character in *Armed for Action*. It was kind of nice to wear a suit and look all dressed up and to play like a mob boss and play the kind of tough guy. It was terrific, I really enjoyed that." All those things are true. That's how I should have handled that. I didn't. I was a schmuck and too carried away with my ego. Both things are honest, but there's two sides to that coin. I felt bad about that since I did it. Rightfully so, David Winters never hired me for another movie and I don't blame him. I wouldn't either. I wouldn't trust the guy with the press.

Going back to *Soultaker*, is it true that Charlie Sheen would dress as Soultaker on Halloween?

I don't know, but let's say I hope so. I've heard that from someplace before. That would be a compliment. I hope that he did. Let's just say that he did.

Tell me about the first time you met Robert Z'Dar.

I met him on set. He came in late because he's always late. We're preparing a shot and here he comes, all 6' foot of him. Bobby was into bodybuilding then. They had dyed his hair blond. He had that big, magnificent jaw. He's all dressed in black. I just thought, "Oh my God, he looks like the grim reaper himself." He looked marvelous, otherworldly. Frankly, I was intimidated. We shook hands and started to talk about the scene. I fell in love with him immediately. He's such a giving actor. And he's an actor, not a personality. He's a real actor. He's a damned good actor. We started talking about just the mechanics of the shoot, how we were going to play this scene, how we were going to block it and such. When we got into that, he was an actor, I was an actor. We were both wanting the same thing, which was make the scene as good as we possibly could. He was terrific in the scene. He got me to be as good as I could in the scene. We have been friends ever since.

That was shot in Mobil, Alabama. You could shoot a film about Mobil in itself. Very southern. It still has those southern traditions, some of which are great and some of which aren't so good. Bobby was much more visible than I was. He had already done *Tango and Cash* (1989) and some other big movies. He was recognizable. Because Bobby would treat everybody as an equal, everybody as a friend, it became a much more relaxed set than it otherwise could have been. He was really an asset for the film.

What's your favorite Z'Dar memory?

We're doing a show called *Point Dume* (1995). It's one helluva film. It's probably the best work that Bobby and I have done individually in the same film together. It shows up now and then, but there's another film that really deserved a lot more than what it got. Performance-wise it's a very intense film with a marvelous plot. We're doing a scene where either I'm going to shoot him or he's going to jump off this 60-foot ledge. He's brilliant. He's absolutely brilliant playing in this movie. He goes from a badass killer to abject coward. Just in shooting that scene and how his transition went from bad guy to just coward. That's what I remember about Bobby, his work as an actor. As a party boy, that would be the Philippines. Did I tell this story before about when we were doing *Double Blast* in the Philippines? This is back in his randy days, which lasted a long time. Wherever Bobby's hotel room was, that was party central. Bobby not only spent his entire Per Diem, but his whole salary on the shoot. But Bobby was great, he was a fun guy. I thank God that when I met Bobby I already stopped drinking; otherwise, I don't think I'd be here today. But in the Philippines with Linda Blair and myself and Bobby, the house of ill repute there; the house of prostitution. One of 'em was called "the fire-house" and the girls used to visit Bobby. But Bobby, just because we were there a number of months, just moved in to "the firehouse." He literally moved into "the firehouse." That was great. I worked with Bobby in Poland. He used to be a bodybuilder. The guy was like a freaking Adonis. But like the rest of us, he got older. But Bobby has always been a gentle soul and he would not hurt a fly. He was the one who introduced me to William Smith. He doesn't drink anymore, thank God, because he wouldn't be with us anymore. I've been with Bobby where he's just been so totally beyond from his drinking and carousing and he was always a good actor, but now he's focused. Hopefully, we've got another good ten years in us.

When did Z'Dar give you the "milkman" nickname?

We were doing *Double Blast* over in the Philippines. There was a scene that I thought deserved a lot more attention than Bobby and Chuck Williams did. I think these guys wanted to wrap. I was trying to make this metaphor about this train going along the tracks. I was kind of being very thoughtful with the scene. "There's a train going across the tracks…" Then Bobby said, "Oh, Christ, Estevez. The milkman!" From then on, it stuck. I show up on the set in Poland and they say, "Hey, the milkman!" Ever since then that's one of my nicknames. That's all right. When the scene came out, I thought it was pretty good. Bobby was terrific in it. I don't know if you've seen

Double Blast, but it's Linda Blair, Bobby and I. It's a good movie. It's a kid's movie. It's fun and funny.

We actually watched it on the set of *Mob Daze* (2002).

You did? Ah, cool. If you didn't like it then lie to me and tell me you loved it.

I actually like the main guy a lot, Dale "Apollo" Cook. I like a lot of his stuff, too.

Oh, really? It seemed like there were two movies. There was this fight stuff. Then there was the bad guy stuff. He's a good guy. I wonder what ever happened to him.

He owns several schools now and was coaching for the league Chuck Norris created. I had called him to be in *Zombiegeddon*. It seemed possible since he wasn't working and was local. He told me he gets an insanely large rate because he's big in Germany.

Wow. When we were in the Philippines, he had billboards. It was because he was a champion and was a white guy, which was a big deal. Good guy. I liked him. I would tell him and the kids, "Please, do not kick me." I remember that. I'd tell them every scene. "Do not hit me. Film is two dimensional, not three." They never did, which I was very happy with.

How do you see yourself being treated by *Mystery Science Theater 3000*?

They did this latest edition and they called me up and asked if I wanted to do an interview. I did. That was absolutely fine. We went out to the park and I did an interview for them, which I think is in what they released. It's just the nature of the beast. That's fine. I think *Soultaker* got a lot more play than it would have if it didn't go on *Mystery Science Theater 3000*. I wish that they wouldn't have cut it up. I wish that they would have shown the whole movie. I think that the movie deserved better. Whoever owned the movie—

somebody had to sign it over to them—that was their choice and they did it. I just made the best of the situation. In a way, it made me more popular. In a way, it hurt the movie.

We talked earlier that they were rather kind to you personally.

Oh, yeah, to me personally they were very nice. When I first came on the scene in the movie, they said, "There's Joe Estevez, the lesser known but more talented brother of Martin Sheen." Wow, man, let me record that. I thought that was very sweet. For me as an actor, they were very kind to me. Any movie that is on there, it's open season on ridiculing it. Most audiences, if you tell them something's good, they'll think it's good. If you tell them something's bad, they'll think it's bad. They don't know how to think. I don't know what good art is. My wife is an excellent artist. To me, I look at Picasso and I look at her stuff and I say, "Hey, I think she's as good as Picasso." I don't know what makes great art. I don't think the lay person out there knows the difference between a good actor and a mediocre actor. I certainly didn't when I was a kid until I really got into acting. You could take *The Wild One* (1953) with Marlon Brando and you could tear Marlon Brando apart. Some of those scenes, by today's standards, are so freaking over the top. That's Marlon Brando, who many people say is the greatest actor who ever lived. I'm not going to argue with that. You can do it with anybody. I realized that as an actor, that once it's put out into the public you get all this criticism. I'd be lying if I didn't say it hurt, but I realize the source. I've also gotten marvelous compliments on movies that I had forgotten about. One of them being *Together and Alone* (1998) by Duane Whitaker. People now are calling it a minor classic. It's just a terrific little movie. I just went in for a day or two and I'm getting rave reviews for it. If it's a classic and you're in it, you're a classic actor. If it's a dud and you're in it, you're a dud actor. A lot of it is really out of my control.

Most of the movies you mention as being good or underrated have been dramas or comedies. Most of the ones that have taken criticism have been horror or sci-fi. Do you feel this has an impact on criticism?

Yeah, but not as a general rule. With horror, it's an international language. If you do a horror film, you stand a pretty good chance of it being sold all over the world. You stand a chance of making some bucks on your movie. That's why filmmakers will choose horror instead of another subject. It's not that they're big horror fans, but that they think they can make this fairly inexpensively and maybe recoup some bucks for it. I've done some horror films that I'm very proud of.

I think that horror films often go for the shock and the horror. When I'm doing a horror film, it's "Okay, that's the field I'm playing in and that's what I'm going to do." As an actor, what do I prefer? Films like *PrimeMates* (2010). Films like *Jumping for Joy*. Films like *Doonby*. Films like *Together and Alone*. Every actor feels that way. We have to make a living. Still, I enjoy the hell out of that character as I'm doing it. I'd much rather do that than say those seven magic words, "Would you like fries with that hamburger?" It's either that or working at McDonald's.

When you made *Zombiegeddon*, you made it for a specific audience. It's almost an acquired taste. The people who go to the horror conventions and stuff, they love *Zombiegeddon*. That's on their must-see. *Dead in Love* (2009) is a brilliant film. *Zombiegeddon* is a cult film for a cult audience. I think most of the people that like *Zombiegeddon* I think might get bored with *Dead in Love*. If I'm doing *The Remnant* (2001), I know the audience that it'll play for. That film did very well, by the way. It's hard to judge an audience, what they're going to like and not going to like. A lot of the cult film audience likes the film to be kind of campy. They enjoy that about it. It's why I enjoy Ed Wood. I love that stuff. Look at the big picture and you have the tombstones falling over—I love it. It's great stuff, but if you get someone off the street I don't think they'd appreciate it the way it should be appreciated. Johnny Depp saw the appreciation in it. Ed Wood's a filmmaker, I appreciate that. I appreciate Conrad Brooks and all the Ed Wood movies he did, the Don Jackson movies that he did. The character that he is. All these conventions and Conrad is still a favorite among them. To have a Conrad Brooks picture and signature, that's something that goes on the wall. For mainstream pictures and such, Conrad

Brooks didn't fare too well. You have to take everything in the context it was delivered. You have to take everything as it was meant to be.

Would you say that *Mystery Science Theater 3000* is responsible for a large portion of your popularity?

I did get a bump up from that, yeah. My daughter Amanda was salivating for the DVD set. They gave me that and I gave it to her— it's still her prized possession. There are fans out there. She grew up with that stuff. It certainly helped. My wife, Connie, loves it. I think it helped people realize I'm somebody besides Martin Sheen's brother. So, it has.

Have you ever felt your name was exploited?

Yeah, but then again that's the name of the game. Anybody that has any sort of name, it's going to be exploited. I've got a couple of letters of intent out there where they're using my name to raise money. I guess that's exploiting me. That's okay. If they get the movie, then they'll pay what I deserve to be paid. There's exploitation that's good and then there's that other type of exploitation. There are movies on my IMDb that somebody chopped together that I never did, exploiting me and some other actors. It's the nature of the beast. I think by my name being exploited, I've benefitted from it. In being connected to my nephew Charlie Sheen, the stories and gossip they make up makes me incredibly angry. They exploited me to sell their gossip and garbage. That I hate, but there's nothing I can do about it.

I want to give you some random titles and actors. Tell me what comes to mind. Let's start with Richard Norton.

Joe and Richard Norton clowning around on the set of *Mind Games*. Courtesy of Adrian Carr.

I love Richard. I think, like with Bobby Z'Dar how people see the jaw and don't realize this guy can act, I think Richard Norton is such a marvelous martial artist that they don't realize he's a marvelous actor. He doesn't get work nearly enough as an actor and star. He's done very well as a martial arts expert, working with Jackie Chan who loves him. He's right at the top of the game there. I think he's also an excellent actor and totally underrated. I love Richard a whole lot. I hope we get to work together a couple more times before we move on to whatever's next.

Fred Olen Ray.

Fred's a good guy. He's quirky. He does wrestling and stuff. He's always treated me well. He's a good guy. I went to a couple of parties over at his house. It's kind of funny, Fred and I were friends and then the last fifteen or so years I haven't heard a peep from him. If he has a problem with me, I certainly hope not. He just stopped calling me. I've seen him a time or two at a convention or AFM. I always liked Fred as a person. He's a very unique guy.

Bloodslaves of the Vampire Wolf (1996).

Conrad Brooks! Oh, yes. That was fun, I enjoyed it. I remember the scene. I go up to him, "My gosh, you're Conrad Brooks! Can I have your autograph?" He says, "You're Joe Estevez!" We had kind of a celebrity stand-off. You know Conrad. Everybody loves Conrad. He was one of the staple players of Don Jackson's. He introduced me to James Chean for *Silent Scream*. He's been very good to me. We did *Baby Ghost* (1995) together for Don Jackson. What a guy. Conrad's a legend. He's one of those guys that make it sweet to be an actor. One of those people I was honored to know. Always has a good thing to say. He's a real find. I'm glad that I have him in my stable of friends.

This story was related to me by Conrad. As Don Jackson does, he was doing some guerilla shooting. He rented a hotel room. Don asked Conrad to put himself in black face like Eddie Cantor did back in the day. Don Jackson in his great, magical genius mind thought it'd be a good idea. So, Conrad's got all this black face and going around the hotel drinking his coffee waiting to film. As luck would have it, there's a group of black gang members at the hotel because it wasn't a four-star place. They saw Conrad in black face. These guys are already pissed off. This just put the match to the fuse. I don't know if you have experienced Conrad when he's being confronted, but he's not the type to back down. It's comical in the sense of looking back because they could have killed the guy. Conrad is explaining to these gang members that he's an actor. Not only is this part of the character, but he has every right given to him by Shakespeare to sit here and be in black face. If you don't like it, you can go straight to hell. As the story goes, and I think I'm clear on this, Scott Shaw was there. Not only is Scott into the Zen and all of that stuff, but he's like a major black belt plus he knows how to use these samurai swords and all this kind of stuff. The story I get is when it reached its crescendo, Scott interjected. In that quiet and peaceful voice of his, told these gang members, "If you don't back off, I will cut your fucking heads off. Look in my eyes 'cause you know that I mean it." Conrad Brooks is still with us. Conrad would not back down an inch.

Conrad Brooks, John Estevez, Constance and Joe Estevez.
Courtesy of Brian Wilson.

Duane Whitaker.

Very talented. I saw *Eddie Presley* (1992). I play his dad in that one. I was just there for a cup of coffee, one scene. When I saw that movie, which is about three days long, he's incredible. Duane Whitaker is an incredible actor. Good guy. He cast me in *Together and Alone*. It's a marvelous film. It's like four o'clock in the morning in Hollywood. No drugs, no drinking, no prostitution—just actors. It's really a melancholy film. It's very moving and in black and white. I was amazed by his talents as a director, writer, and actor. That guy has the whole package. The only thing he needs, like you need, is some money to work with. Talented guy. Like all of us, he just needs to work more. It's not his fault, but he just needs to work more.

Demolition Highway (1996).

With Danny Fendley, he was the star of it. I had a ball doing it. Danny Fendley was just great. Danny was a big deal then in Atlanta. We worked in about four different states and he owned about six different hotels. We'd drive to another state and stay in his hotels. It was great fun. I've been a friend with Danny ever since that movie. The twins who played my two bodyguards are still my very best friends. I got a lot of friends and great memories from that movie.

Werewolf (1996).

Tony Zarindast was the director. I think that's also on *Mystery Science Theater 3000*. I went in there and did my job. I think I did pretty good. Mike Tristano was doing the weapons on that and brought me in. It was fun. I just did another movie for Tony last year. He's Iranian. Their idea of a good film in Iran is totally different than what they think of as a good film here. I mean that. What we might think is campy, they think is cool. It's very two dimensional. There's not a lot of depth or nuances, at least the films I'm familiar with. Tony paid me what he said he was going to pay me and I had fun. So, it was good.

Michael Madsen.

I like Michael. I like him. He's like all of us and has his demons. I think that a couple of those demons might get out of control every now and then. He's an excellent actor. I don't think even he realizes how good he is. He's a great dad. He's got an incredible amount of bills he has to pay which I think leads him to do movies he otherwise wouldn't do. I like working with Michael. I've seen him a couple of times since I've worked with him and he's been nothing but a gentleman and very kind to me. We've done at least two movies together. Mike's a good guy. The stuff that comes out in the press...you got to watch yourself a little bit. I think Mike sometimes lets it slip away. You have to understand you're a public person. What he does in public he's not going to get away with like the average guy. He's a terrific actor and I'm proud to have worked with him.

Marc Dacascos.

Good guy. I worked with him in *No Code of Conduct* and then worked with him in Serbia on a film. Great, real person. Hard, hard worker. He's got a body like a stone. He's one of those martial artists, too. He hosts *Iron Chef* (2004), I think. Good looking guy, an excellent actor. I think that if he weren't half-Asian and all white, he'd be working more in mainstream as a leading actor. I think because he's part Asian, he gets typecast as that. Even in the movie we did in Serbia, it was two brothers—he and Michael Madsen—and they had to make it half-brothers. I think that hurts him. He's got a helluva lot of things going for him. He's done very well. He's someone that I hope to work with down the road. He's very, very giving. He's very vulnerable. A lot of actors aren't. They play their characters close to the chest. He is very giving and I appreciate him for it.

What is your opinion of casting directors?

If you're a good actor, they should call you in. If you're not, if you're not right for it, it shouldn't have anything to do with this nonsense, you know? Now, I have a friend who found something in the breakdown that he really wanted to be submitted for and he called his agent to call the casting director and he said, "No, I'm not gonna call her because I might make her angry and then she's not going to call me when there's something that is good for my clients, she's going to quit calling me." The power that these guard dogs at the door have is ludicrous.

When I worked in a factory I was a troublemaker in the factory because I just had a problem with authority and people telling me what to do that I didn't want to do. And I had a problem with the casting directors being authority. I still have a problem, but now I'm my own boss. So, I'm pretty well a happy guy, but my wife has the same problem. I never dare tell her what to do because she lets me know about it. It's just this unreasonable authority. People can tell you what to do just because somebody has given them something that signifies authority. It's absolutely ludicrous. We're fastly becoming a police state here. We have so many people and so many rules that you have to abide by. I guess it's the nature of the beast and so the clamps are coming down ever stronger with every passage of every little law.

So I was kind of in no man's land, and I got called in for this movie called *South of Reno* (1988). It was a big-time casting director, Ann Ramsen, whose daughter is a pretty popular actor. So, I went in, I auditioned and I got the part. It became kind of a minor classic. It was kind of in the vein of *Blood Simple* (1984). It was an independent film. Just the freedom that I had to have dialogue with the director, and that he would actually listen to me and incorporate my ideas into the scene. I said, "Man, this is what it's about." And TV and sitcoms, they won't let you change a word. Not because what you say is worse. What you say is often better, but it's not what the writer wrote and oftentimes the writer is often the producer. So, you're not gonna change his thing, no matter what, you know? That's just the way it is. They've got the power and Hollywood is all about power.

If I might digress, with my nephew Charlie. He did this thing with *Two and a Half Men*. Okay, the timing was not good. But, having said that just the show itself, *Two and a Half Men*, I can understand the frustration. I can understand his frustration with the producers and executive producers. Whatever else you can say about Charlie, I believe he's an incredibly talented actor. My wife may disagree, but I think he's an incredibly talented actor. He's got a marvelous imagination and to not be able to use that imagination, he may as well be at that frigid air factory in Dayton, Ohio, because he's not even given a chance to flower. If you don't have a chance to progress than you digress and I think that's how he digressed back into the booze and the debauchery. And there's always that money as the bait. They threw so much money at him for *Two and a Half Men*. How could a sane man turn that down? I mean, maybe he should have turned that down because maybe he wouldn't have had to go through that backstabbing. Now he's sober again, God bless him. Good for him. TV is stifling, it's stifling. It's incredibly stifling for me. It's not, as an actor, you need to create. And I wasn't creating. You're just a rope there. You're just hitting your mark and saying your lines. You get in a canned laugh from the audience and, okay, move on. It's all about commercialism. It's all about selling that product in between the cheap bits, you know? So, I never felt comfortable with TV. When I landed that part in *South of Reno*, it just opened the world to me. And people started telling me, "Hey, man, you're a helluva actor." It's like, wow, if I'm getting to do what I want to do, I can work my art here. I can work my trade in independent film.

So, that's the movie that sparked your love for independent film?

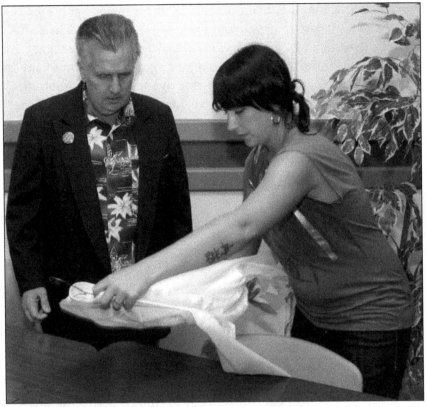

Joe looks over wardrobe. Shot by Steve Thompson, © Brett Kelly.

That is, then I got a movie called *Retreads* (1988), which was eight weeks in extreme location in Wisconsin with a couple of crackheads who were the producers. That was really interesting working with these guys. But I got to ride a motorcycle and be a tough guy. It was a great experience. Then, shortly after that, I got *Soultaker*. *Soultaker* kind of made me a viable name. Back in the day, and this was all videotape and mom and pop stores and videotapes and such, *Soultaker* did very well among the independent film crowd and that's just when independents were making their mark, by the way. So I became kind of an independent film actor name. It's like being a great baseball player in Cuba. You do okay, Fidel takes care of you, but you're not going to make the money the big boys make back in the States. But I was in hog heaven. From *Soultaker* on I was pretty much working. And I still am working. I've done a lot of movies that, looking back on it, I should not have done, but, you know, I'm an actor. I don't know the final outcome of these movies, but I know that I like this part, I get to say these words and this check has cleared the bank and I get to pay my rent with money I've made as an actor. I'm kind of a meat-and-potatoes guy. If I've got a couple bucks in the bank to take care of me for the next couple of months, I'm in heaven. I'm doing okay, you know. I've always had that factory worker's mentality, you know? I've never really aspired to make big dollars. I've never really thought that, so that's been my mentality throughout. I worked with Jeff Conaway, he passed away. I got to work with a lot of actors. Big name actors. I don't want to say on the way down, but after TV used them up and spit them out. And then, you know, you do that series and your phone's not ringing anymore. And then, they come into independent films. But it's surprising that you know an actor gets a reputation as a TV actor. That's not an international reputation. So, for an independent filmmaker, he's not as bankable sometimes as someone like me. I mean, Erik Estrada is an international name, he's gonna work, Jeff Conaway's gonna work because he's an international name. But, Dustin Diamond, I did *Little Creeps* with him and he's a funny guy, great actor. But, he was on that show *Saved By the Bell* seven years or whatever, but he doesn't have any international name, you know? He's not recognized in Czechoslovakia, Poland or Serbia.

Kind of like David Faustino, too. I always thought he was great.

I always thought *Married...with Children* was a fantastic show. And he's great. He's funny; he's right off the cuff. I love to work as an actor. I like to improvise and ad-lib and he's right there with me. He's marvelous. Some actors will only work from a script and they don't want to ad-lib. They don't want to improvise and I understand that. That's okay. But, I mean, there's a lot of magic that happens in the moment and I like to take advantage of that because it only happens once and then it's gone. If you're sitting there doing a scene and somebody farts, you better do something with that. You only get that opportunity once especially if it's you that's farting. But, stuff happens and it's magic and if you run with it and nothing happens, they do another take. That's what's marvelous about it.

Joe Estevez being interviewed. Courtesy of Blake Fitzpatrick

But he was on that series for like eight years and because that was a big show, I thought this guy's got money. He could live forever, but there are no residuals. He's got nothing. That's why he's out there banging around in the independent scene.

Independent movies opened up doors, but they also involve an element of chaos. What's the most insane story you've been involved with in an independent movie?

I tell you just because I'm trying to get it off of my mind. There's just this mad thing that I just did in Houston. I've been a professional actor for 37 years. I'm not a quitter. I have stuck with every movie until I was finished with it. I often say that acting in a movie is kind of like having sex. Even the worst sex I've ever had wasn't bad. Worst movie I ever did wasn't bad. I still enjoyed myself. It was great fun. I made a big mistake. I signed on to direct this movie called *Inside Out*—I'd worked with the producer before. I just did a couple of days on two of his films. The director, Brenton Covington, brought me in. I had a great time and it was in Phoenix. I came back and said to the producer, "I'd like to direct one of your films." Well, unfortunately, he called me. And I went to Brenton Covington and said, "I don't want to take this gig from you." He said, "Oh no. I read that script and turned it down." I said, "Oh no." It's a horrible script and it's gonna be a horrible movie, but it's gonna be my horrible movie. Because there are a lot of things we have when you have a vision. And there are certain scenes where you can work your muse and magic in. And even if the whole movie doesn't play well, you got these four or five scenes that really played well and are magic. So that's what I went into it for. Now, Connie told me,

"Read the writing on the wall, Joe," when the first thing that happened, they promised me x amount of dollars. Three thousand dollars for expenses. I called and I said, "Are you sure this is expenses? I get this money?" And the day before I'm leaving the executive producer said, "Oh no. That's for your plane ticket and your car." But I still went. I should have smelled a rat right then. I got there and apparently he was looking for a cheerleader. I had no say in casting. I had no say in locations. All that was done before I got there.

How limited was your input in the film?

I had no say in anything. But at least I'm going to direct. We go out to locations. She doesn't have a location. She has a street, we'll shoot here. "Well, aren't there people living here?" "Oh, don't worry, we'll shoot here." So, I had a cameraman that was going to do the whole film in steadicam. Unfortunately, I'm not a technical person. If I ever direct again, I need a cameraman like a John Soujin that I've worked with before that can really cover my backside. The first thing I shot with this cameraman, I said I just want to pan down and pick up the actor coming from the mausoleum. He said, "Oh, I can't do that." I said, "Excuse me." He said, "Oh no, no, no."

"But I have seen this shot done a thousand times while I had been on the set to see it."

"Well, that's from a much more experienced cameraman and I just don't know how to do that."

We didn't have a dolly. We had nothing. We had this little Cannon 57A-something. That was it. He was going to mount that on a steadicam and shoot the whole movie. So, we're working two days and I never knew this about myself. With this and that I am the nicest guy in the world. Man, I'm smiling all the time, drinking my Diet Coke. I'll take a jog at lunch, you know. I'm fine. I piss and moan now and then, but it's all good natured. I was a raving madman lunatic on that set. They have a big industry over there to shoot the oil industrials and everybody that was left over, that never got a job, ended up on this film. And it was like walking zombies. Everybody that was on this film, it was the first time they were doing what they were doing—whether it was props or scripts or

A.D. or camera. So, this script, it's lunacy. He told me he's a very mediocre writer. Second day here and I find myself a real cheerleader with the actors. I baby them. But with everybody else, I asked for some of the simplest things and they just sit there. Fuck it, I'll get it myself. And I'm getting bricks out of the frickin' alley for the girl to stand on so I can get people together because I don't have so much—just the basics about creating a scene for the screen and then actors they don't know. They don't know to see the eyes rather than the profile. In independent movies, you've got to see the eyes because you're getting very little coverage. So don't waste anything on profile. Get the eyes and as few setups as possible to tell that story and a few coverage shots and get out of there because you're doing ten pages a day because you don't have the time to be Orson Welles.

How did you cope with the chaos?

Pick your battles, pick your scenes. I would find the one I want to work some magic in and you pace yourself where you can give that scene two and a half hours. So, it's the last scene on the second day and it's like I'm doing this whole thing myself. Literally, I'm doing this whole thing myself. And there's this scene that was supposed to be on a scooter, but it wasn't. It was on a walker so I just changed the dynamics of it. And I thought it was terrific. I thought just the depth of this young lady as an actress and, wow, this was just a piece of poetry and that was the last scene of the day and I get to spend about two and a half hours on it. So I could sculpture it. I said this is my little jewel, "Forget the movie, folks, just watch this part." And so the producer said, "All right, let's just shoot it the way it was written." I said, "No, no. This is what I want, this is fine." She said, "The executive producer wants to shoot it the way it is in the script." I said, "I'm not going to do that because if I do that you'll use that and you won't use this and I don't want to give you the choice." That's a wrap. That was Friday night; I said, "I'll see you all Sunday." So, I went back to the hotel and they shot the scene the way the producer had written it. I was beside myself with madness. And the producer just happened to be coming into town. And I'm just screaming. I'm begging to be fired. I'm extremely upset. "You guys are clowns. This isn't motion picture making. This is your egos speaking. You want this monstrosity on the screen for what? This is nonsense. I'm not gonna do it and fire me." So part of the deal of me directing was that I had to be in the movie so the next day was all about me. And even then we've got two scenes going this way and I said to the cameraman, "No, no, man we've got to finish it out this way first before we turn the cameras around." So I was acting, so I was fairly well faking it that day. I went in there and I said, "I'm going to do this my way." That day went badly. The next day, I said I'll just try it their way. I'll just be an acting coach.

What was your reaction to that approach?

It was miserable. I hated myself for being there and I had a talk with myself and the only reason why I was there was to get paid. That was it. And I said, "I can't work. I can't do that. I can't work just, that makes me a whore. Let these other people be whores. I came in here to direct. I know the movie's garbage, I know that. But I came in here to direct." So, I called the producer and said, "I'm sorry. I'm not your whipping boy anymore. The first day we're three hours late because of the camera and he forgot the cards back at the hotel." And the first thing the producer says to me is, "Okay, you're three hours late. Get the day, get the day." And everything, which I didn't know is the director's fault. So I was, like, okay. I'm okay, you know. You're like a quarterback, it goes well. So, the next days, I got my days. But I could have got more. So, you're never gonna please anyone. And there were a lot of Indians from Bollywood on this movie. I didn't want to do a Bollywood movie. Like six days, four days, they try to set records over there on how fast they can do a movie. That was the first movie that I ever quit and I quit. I just said, "I can't do this."

How far was it into the movie that you quit?

Like halfway. The lady who was the producer was also a director, using that term very, very loosely. So, it wasn't like I was leaving them in the lurch. She could take the money that she was paying me and pay it back on herself. I felt bad and, still, I'd go out and talk to myself and jog and say, "Did I do the right thing?" And I did the right thing, but oftentimes just because you do the right thing doesn't mean you don't feel bad.

It was a nightmare. I have been on some pretty amateur independent films, but every film I had been on, that producer and that director wanted to make the best possible film. This film in Houston, that wasn't the case. They were making this thing where it was some kind of homage to this executive-producer guy. He had won on one of his films a Houston International Film Festival award. I don't know if you know about the Houston International Film Festival award. For all you folks out there in reading land understand this about the International Houston Film Festival award: if you've got a piece of garbage, but you want to win an award, take it to the Houston International Film Festival. They will give you an award. It might cost you a little bit more money, but they will give you an award. But don't put this award on the wall because anybody that sees that knows that you're stupid. So, this guy has on his wall this Houston International Film Festival award. I couldn't help myself. I could have, but I didn't. I explained to him about only idiot first-time filmmakers have the stupidity to hang that from their wall, because the Houston International Film Festival is a rip-off. It is a rip-off. It is a moneymaking machine for the guy that organized this. And I'll tell that to the guy's face and he knows it and he's making a kazilllion dollars every year from independent filmmakers that want to get some, which they should, "attaboys" for their film. You need some attaboys. Don't go to Houston. It's a waste of money and everybody knows that award is just not worth the little cellophane it's written on. But that's what the guy had on his wall and he proclaimed himself a brilliant filmmaker because look at this award.

What's your most memorable award experience?

I got an award which was kind of cumulative with the Queen's Film Festival. They brought me in as a special guest and they gave me a lifetime achievement award, year before last. And I thought, "Wow, how sweet." And you know, we get awards and we get things throughout the years, but that one I kept. And it's on my mantle along with the plaque they gave me because that award it means something to me and it was kind of like it was a recognition from fellow independent filmmakers that said, "You're one of us and we like you and you like us and here's a little something to show that." And that meant and still means a lot to me. We independent filmmakers, and there's a lot of us—I worked in twelve foreign countries on independent films. We are everywhere. We are all over the world and we've got something to say and we're trying to use this medium in film to say it with. I applaud every one of them.

Do you think filmmakers can elicit a change in society?

Absolutely, especially the filmmakers that try to use this vehicle as their platform to speak from. I think something happened back in the '70s where we had an opportunity to change this world. Back during the movement where we were so anti-war and the flower children and I came of age during that time. And there was a power in this country to do something. Some people tried, but most of them just took the money and ran. Most of them just sold their art out to the highest bidder. And in doing that, sold our country out because we as artists are nothing more than the court jesters. The one that sits at the throne of the king and tells him in a humorous way what's wrong with him and his kingdom so he won't chop off our heads, but take it home, think about it, and maybe make some changes. That's our place in this society. But we opted out for the money and I think that because we haven't disciplined ourselves and we gave into the drugs—John Belushi was a great talent. You gotta take that talent and you've got to discipline and you've got to hone it and then it flowers. But, if you get into the drugs, you're as Jesus Christ said in the Bible, "You're the seed that fell upon the rock." You grow for a little while, but then you just curl up and die. You don't receive any water. And I think we as a generation, my generation, we betrayed this nation. And we betrayed the younger filmmakers that are coming after us. But I ask these younger film-makers that are coming up now, because there are so many things wrong with this world. There is so much that needs to be corrected

Richard Norton and Adrian Carr [director] with Joe. Courtesy of Adrian Carr.

and they have a pulpit from that viewfinder inside that camera, that's your pulpit. And you can change the world. Your films. That's why you were given the passion to make this film. Don't do like our generation did and opt out for the biggest bucks. You got in this business for something to say. Say it. Because life is short, man. And if you trust yourself as an artist, there's always gonna be money there. Not a lot, but there's gonna be monies there to take care of yourself. You're always going to have something to eat and a place to sleep. That's all you really need when it comes down to it: food, clothing and shelter. Everything else is expressing yourself. So express that flame that is in your heart because you can. You actually can change the world. Look what one person did: Gandhi. Look what one person did: Martin Luther King. For his short time on the stage, look what President Jack Kennedy did. Your films are important. But you can't give into the temptation of big bucks and mediocrity. You've got to be true to the passion that made you an artist in the first place. Not just a bean counter that is selling your soul to the highest bidder. So, that's my preaching the gospel to the filmmakers.

Did that last experience sour you on directing or will you do it again with your own passion project?

It soured me. If I direct again, I just have to have all my people in the departments and I'll have to cast it. As an actor, as a director, I'm very vulnerable playing these characters. I'm wearing my heart on my sleeve. And I'm only screaming at the different departments because they're not giving the respect these actors need to get in order to give the scenes some kind of justice they deserve. These actors are pouring their hearts out, their emotions. Silence, dammit, let me have an audition with these actors. Let me at least have one audition. I get three seconds, then it's like, clang, clang. So, I can't because I'm vulnerable. I can't put myself back into that kind of a situation. And I don't want to do any kind of film that is spiritually negative. It has to have some kind of a redeeming quality; that a person who is watching this movie can leave and be a better person for it. At least maybe have a few thoughts that are positive from it. You can do that with a zombie movie, with a horror movie, with a love interest movie. You can do that with any kind of movie.

I'm glad you have that outlook because a lot of people bastardize certain genres of film, such as horror.

I did a movie last year where I played a social worker. He was a social worker by day and he was unable to make any difference in the world. So, he takes it upon himself to go out and take care of these people at night that are being mean to these children. I thought there's a lot of redeeming stuff in this. It's like, bastard, you pay for what you're doing to this kid. Pay for it. You go through the system and get your hand slapped, but no. You actually got to pay. I take out this baseball bat to make them pay. This is rent due right here. But I thought there was a moral redemption from that. So, yeah. I think that these movies that are out there, these people are taking money to give to charity and make these better than thou movies. Come on! You're preaching to the choir, first of all. You've got to reach down in and get those guys that otherwise wouldn't be able to hear a good word. This whole life to me is a salvation. And that word is to salvage. To salvage yourself. We all, every one of us, we've all had our crosses to bear. That's a given. But with these scars and with these outrageous fortunes we have, do something anyway. Do something good even if you're feeling that bad. Do something good with it anyway. Jesus, Quasimodo was able to ring the bell. You can be a force for good. There are so many Paris Hiltons.

What don't you like about Paris Hilton?

I'm sorry. I think she is a force for evil. I use evil and maybe I should substitute that word as a force for negative. People are rewarded for being negative. She's being rewarded for giving head to a guy in a home movie porn film and now she's on top of the world and she's worshipped. That's not what your society should be about. We should say to that, "Young lady, that's not what you're on this planet for." But she's celebrating herself and all this materialism and we are about all this materialism. I'm watching TV the other night and these commercials come on. And what do these commercials have to do with what I was just watching? Well, okay, they pay for what I was just watching. But, wait a minute. I pay for my TV, I pay for my cable, I pay for my electricity. Shouldn't that have been paid for? I am basically a socialist. And I don't know where that became a bad word. And I don't know when in the hell capitalism became a good word. People don't understand. Capitalism, a capitalist here in this country and every other place around the world, they owe their allegiance to no country. They owe their allegiance to one thing: making money. And they will take every fucking penny you've got. And then kick you to the curb and go to somebody else that's got money. It's supposed to be a good thing, as if our founding fathers who signed that Declaration of Independence welcome in capitalism as a way to run this society. That's not the way it was and that's not the way it should be right now.

How do you feel society should be run?

We are human beings; we are our brothers' keepers. When somebody else is suffering, you should be suffering. And you only find relief in giving them relief. That is what being a human being is about. A human being is not about having more than somebody else, or being in comfort while somebody else suffers. I'm an old man already. I just got here and I'm an old man already. How the hell did that happen? I just turned around and I'm an old man. So, I'm just saying to the people that are reading this or hearing it, time goes by so very quickly and you find yourself old before you know it. You'd better look back and say to yourself, "I hope I did something that had some real worth, something that had some real worth. That added to this humanity." Other than just being a useless, I love this term, I'm sorry: a useless fuckin' food eater. And that's what most of these people are. They just gobble up shit. I often say to my wife, 80 percent of the people that are working, just send them home. Pay 'em, just send 'em home. Because they're useless. They're just guardians at the door. They don't do anything but prevent real things from happening. They're just guard dogs at the door. Meaningless, useless food eaters.

If you are in an occupation that isn't bettering humanity in some way or another, I guarantee you are in the wrong occupation—you are doing the wrong thing with your life. Readjust yourself, have a drink. Sit down on that back porch, on the curb or whatever and think, "What am I really supposed to be doing here?" These asshole capitalists, they aren't the ones that put you here. I love this question. I put it in the play I love it so much. One of my characters asks this of the other character. He says, "Who are you?" He says, "Well, I'm an actor, you know?" He says, "Who are you?" He says, "I am energy. I am energy. Energy born and sustained by God. I am courage and coward. I am madness and beauty. I am love and hate. I am poetry discombobulating. I am all these things and more." He goes on a little bit longer than that, but that's what you are. You are a song. Sing that song as long as you can and when your time is up, you've done your job and you will die with a smile on your face and you will be worn out. If you live your life saving yourself, for what? For a coffin that's gonna cost more than the guy who's buried next to you? For what? Use yourself up, man. You were born with a good conscience. Listen to it. Listen to that beating of the heart. Listen to that spiritualism that is the world. Listen to the angels. Listen to the leprechauns. Listen to that little dance that's in your mind. Dance barefoot in the street. Rip your shirt off.

So, you believe life should be celebrated to its fullest?

Absolutely. I remember I was doing a gig once in the Cayman Islands and they invited me in to be the pirate king. How they ever got my name or whatever I don't know, but I was a little overweight at the time and it's a British tradition, but the pirates they took over the island and they reenact it every year. I was the pirate king. I came in and took over the island and there was a big parade over main street and it's great, the Cayman Islands. The whole island is a party. And I was fat then. I'm a little fat now, but I was really fat then. I was about 200 pounds. And everybody is dancing in the street. And I was with a friend of mine, Mona. I just tore off my shirt. Went barefoot. Big fat belly and I'm dancing in the street to this reggae music. It's the freest I've ever been in my life. Just free. Just sing that song. Just let your body well up and sing that song. Don't suppress that cry, let it flow, you know? Don't suppress that laugh. Be a laughing hyena. Soak up this life because, man, it just passes so short and all you're left with is regrets and a bank account that the banks are probably gonna go belly up and steal all your money anyway like they just did so live, live. We're here to live. We're here to use ourselves up.

There is a groundswell not with independent movies because people aren't seeing the people who are running the movie theatres. The movies that go into the movie theatres are the bean guys. And these movies are getting more sophomoric and they're made for children. They're not made for people who think. One of the most beautiful movies that my wife and I have ever seen, was a movie called *The Story of the Weeping Camel* (2003). Beautiful, beautiful piece of art. *My Dinner with Andre* (1981). Beautiful piece of art. And if I may say so the movie that Will Wallace and I did, *PrimeMates*, four guys sitting in a smoke shop, smoking cigars. It really got to the humanity of man. What the hell are we doing here, you know? These movies are really starting to get to the surface because people want films to say something. I think that independent films have become more and more popular. And so what if a viewing audience is twenty thousand, or ten thousand? Ten thousand is a hell of a lot of people. I mean, look, the smallest movie you ever made, in the smallest audience out there, is a hell of a lot more people than

Abraham Lincoln ever talked to in his entire life. So, man, you're talking to a lot of people out there and don't take it for granted. You do have something to say. Every human being has something to say. And it may be as simple but profound as "I love you." I love you. That's what life is. "Love one another" was Bob Marley's advice to his children. His total advice about the human experience. Love one another. And love moves mountains.

Tell us about *Doonby*.

If you remember the movie *It's a Wonderful Life* (1946) and if you remember the movie *The Time of Your Life* (1948) with James Cagney; it's a cross between those two. It's about a fellow who comes to town and just because of his very presence, people's lives change. It's a movie about how incredibly important one person can be, and what life would be like if that one person wasn't there. Like Jimmy Stewart standing off the bridge, he's gonna jump and his angel comes along and this is what would happen if he wasn't around. And it's an action-packed movie, it's got some good names in it. Robert Davi, Jennifer O'Neil plays my wife, and John Schneider. That guy can flat-out act. In *Dukes of Hazzard* he's limited to, you know, being good old slick boy. This guy has incredible depth as an actor. And it shines on the screen. And I've told him and I've said in interviews, this guy is going to be with the A-list actors again. And I believe we're getting a 3,000-theatre release, which is incredible. The guy that we have doing publicity, Mark Joseph, is the same guy that did the publicity for *Passion of the Christ* (2004). Here's a movie, no stars, in a different language, which everybody already knew the ending to. This guy is a publicity genius. It is a very impassioned movie and I saw it and I'm pretty critical, I'm very critical of movies I'm in. I'm critical of dead spaces in a film where you're just trying to move the story forward and you have to get out this information. There's none of that. There's no dead spaces. It's an exciting film. I'm one of the leads. It's a marvelous part. I'm very thankful for it. I think that it's certainly not gonna cost me any work.

Is this the movie you're most proud of so far?

I'm very proud of *Doonby*. I'm very proud of *PrimeMates*. There's a lot of movies I'm proud of. *Together and Alone* is a helluva movie. Duane Whitaker is on the list. But I guess it's kind of, it's the latest one that I'm proud of. But it's kind of like old loves. They're the greatest thing since sliced bread at the time, but then they kind of fade in your remembrances as something else. You know, I work with actors and I say, man, I gotta work with this gal or with this guy again or...I'm sure it happens to me. People probably say that about me. I work on other movies and other actors come along and you kind of think that's life. *Doonby's* on the front page now, for me and my mind and I'm very proud of it because it does have something to say and it says it so seamlessly. And I think that's a beautiful moviemaker that can do that.

Did you think differently about actors when you were directing?

I was more protective of them. I know myself as an actor, I can pretty well work by myself and I don't let many distractions bother me. I just stay within myself and save myself to when we're shooting. But, these kids they don't. They get carried away with all the nonsense happening that doesn't have anything to do with their performances. So, I became very protective of them. I feel bad about turning these kids over to the barbarians. But, they may as well learn now as well as later. This is the jungle. If they want to do this for a living, this is the jungle they're gonna have to slay their meat at.

You've been working Fi-Core for awhile now. What's the distinction between it and SAG?

I think Equity is a terrific union, a terrific guild. They really try and make a difference for their actors. SAG, at best, is a dinosaur. I think SAG is totally out of touch with actors and actors' needs. First of all, it's a guild, it's not a union. A union's job is when you're out of work, they help you get work. SAG will never, ever get you a job in your life. Let me take that back. What turned me against SAG was every year they have a competition of the best unshot screenplays. No money behind it, but a great screenplay. And then they do a staged reading of it up at Slamdance which goes on at the same time as Sundance. There was script one year called *The Fourth Round*. Great script, I don't think it's ever been done, but SAG produced this big showing up in Park City, Utah. They flew us up, first class. First-class hotels, arrangements, everything. We were there for three days and they had the most expensive wines, diners, everything. We got Per Diem to put on this little show. All this was paid for by SAG, treating these actors like princes. I like being treated like a prince, that's all good. But I think, all these actors paying whatever the minimum is that they're paying SAG by waiting tables have gone to putting us up here. Same thing with the SAG awards. This has all gone to propagate SAG and to put them up on some kind of pedestal rather than just doing the job that they were initiated to do.

Do you feel like SAG is a counter-productive organization?

I think that when they were first formed, they had a good purpose and it was a good institution. But like all institutions, whether it's the Catholic Church or SAG or General Motors, it starts to decay. And SAG has started to decay and exists to perpetuate itself. There's no concern with the actors. I'm gonna talk out of school about my brother, Martin Sheen, who is a member of the board of SAG. I stopped by his house one day when I had an audition up in Malibu and we're talking back there while he's playing basketball. And he says, "All these independent movies that you do, a lot of them are nonunion, aren't they?" I said, "Yeah." He said, "How do you do that?" I said, "Financial Core." He said, "Financial Core, what's that?" I explained to him briefly what it is. But, that's not the point of the conversation. The point of the conversation is he's an officer of SAG. He should know what Financial Core is. I would bet that there's at least twenty percent of SAG members that have gone Financial Core.

What Financial Core is is that you write a letter to SAG and you say that I want to do any movie that asks me to do it and do the necessary paperwork so that I can do this. What you lose is your right to vote at SAG and you lose your right to run for office. Everything else stays intact. Your pension, your residuals, every-

Courtesy of Scott Shaw.

thing stays perfectly intact. It's the law. SAG is breaking the law by not letting you work nonunion movies. But they don't tell you that because then they're losing that money they're gonna get so they want to discourage filmmakers from making (non-union) films. I think that's a sin. I think any Screen Actors Guild is discouraging filmmakers from making films. What the hell is wrong with this picture? The world's gone completely mad. I would suggest to any actor that's just got their SAG card, the first thing you do is go Fi-Core. You didn't come to Hollywood to be a guild member. You came to Hollywood to act. Remember that. Don't get sidetracked with all this nonsense and these nice, shiny plastic Screen Actors Guild cards that you can show everybody that you're an actor, but you're still waiting tables while the guy who should be waiting tables has taken your part in that independent movie down the street.

When somebody goes Fi-Core, do they need to worry about SAG coming after them?

No. SAG can't do a thing. It's the law. And the person who pushed this through Congress was Charlton Heston. Charlton Heston was a past president of the Screen Actors Guild. And he pushed this through because he saw the injustices of actors who were out of work because of the Screen Actors Guild. They couldn't accept this legitimate job because this company didn't go union. And they can give reasons and details and such but like everything else, it's all about the money. And SAG and those employees, they make a nice salary. Those board members, a nice salary. What about this actor over there that's waiting tables? What's he making?

You have over 200 credits on IMDb. How do you stay so prolific?

Because I've met so many people throughout the country that have asked me to do a picture. I may not do another one for three, four years down the line. But, usually they'll call me back and have something for me, but it's pretty much that I know so many independent filmmakers that usually I'm busy. This year I played the lead in a movie called *Little Creeps*. Last year I played the lead in a movie called *The Vigilante* (2010), but at the age I'm getting now that's rare. Because I'll play a supporting character or the head villain or the head cop and because of that you work three, four days, maybe a week, but you don't get the run of the picture. So that way if normally I'm doing the run of the picture, it's a four-week gig or so. This is a four-week gig. That's why I can do many pictures in a year's time. And usually folks notify me ahead of time whether they want me. I just got a gig yesterday, a movie called *You and Me* that's shooting in February so I'll just make sure that with whatever's happening, I'll be clear to do it when February comes.

Does that much work take a toll on you?

It takes a toll if I'm not working. I get very antsy; I think there's something in me that I have to work. If I'm not doing movies, I'll start writing, which is also a good thing. During the holiday season is when I wrote those two plays and whatever else. And I think when the phone finally does stop ringing I'll spend my time writing.

You mentioned the writing before. Is this a new thing for you?

It is. I had no ego about it before, but I think I'm pretty good at it. My wife's a writer. She's an excellent writer and she's schooled me and I've just kind of been naturally holding myself to it. I enjoy the discipline of it. Not that I enjoy the discipline of it, but the discipline of it is very good for me. And then when I get to the finished product, whether it's a play or a short story, I'm very proud of myself for that. And I think when the time comes in a year or two, I'll do a book.

There's a solitary aspect of writing. Does that bother you since usually you're around a lot of people when you're acting?

I think it kind of complements the other, because I enjoy having the total control. I think I enjoy the total control. Once you finish it you lose control and it's whatever they do with it but I'm always...there's big reasons, way back in the day, I'd get a TV script and I'd change it. They didn't like it. But, it's better this way. It doesn't matter. "Say the words that are there. You're getting paid, say the words that are written there." I found in independent film that I pretty much rewrite everything that I get. Unless it's a good writer, then I'll leave it alone. But, I can't force myself to memorize something until I find that rhythm in it. In a script, in a scene, it has to be like a musical score. And I rewrite it until I find that rhythm and that's what I memorize.

Do you have screenplays written that you want to get out there and market?

No, I couldn't care less about screenplays. I do plays and short stories and I think I've got at least one book in me about Brown Street, the street I grew up in and all the great characters that lived on that street.

Would this be a novel?

It'll be just different episodes, different chapters. And every chapter will be about a different character in the neighborhood. And I think I got more than enough in me for a book on that. So, I think when I'm working, I have an excuse not to write, so I don't really do that but if I've been off for three or four weeks, I get kind of antsy and I feel like I've got to earn my supper. I've got to earn my keep.

How long have you been writing?

Not really that long. Maybe the last seven years.

What raised your interest in doing it?

I just felt an urge to write and my wife Connie, she is just an incredible good news motivator.

What are you really interested in writing about?

I like to take characters that are out of society or out of the normal frame of workaday. I use these characters that can make objective views on the society that we live in rather than subjective views and *Hobos* is absolutely perfect for that because it's outside of the mainstream. So, that to me is a good vehicle. In this art form that we toil in, we're very much outside the mainstream. These people with the lunches and you know this back to work and all, that's something that, thank God, we don't have to do but, I don't know. I see so much out here that's just unhappiness and so much misery and working for the man and not working for themselves. And I just ask the questions: why are we here? What are we doing here? It certainly isn't to work in a factory 40 years and live your life in fear. I think there's a lot of fear we're not born with, but that we inherit or we learn and I don't think it's something that we should encourage in ourselves. I like fear and love, those basic emotions. And madness. I love to write about those things.

We are very capitalistic: an over the top, capitalistic society. Yet, we've convinced all the working masses that that's good, and that socialism is bad. It's just idiocy that we are all really working for the man to make him that much richer while we sit and get poorer. Yet, we fight in Iraq and Afghanistan and all over the world to make sure we keep him in power. It's ludicrous. It's madness. I mean, if you look at society, it is absolutely ludicrous how we live. Two states in the country right now are in massive heat. It's been going on for

26 days. We've had an incredibly horrible winter, the worst winters this country we've ever had. It's obvious global warming. It's obvious. But nobody's saying that. And who's causing the global warming? It's the people that run this country. And they keep cranking out the shit that pollutes the air and causes these methane gases and the oil spills in the gulf, but I love that when Murdoch is testifying, and that guy that threw the pie at his face or tried to was all of us. He was the common man saying, "Take this!" And yet they take the common man away in handcuffs. That says everything to me. That says everything about how upside down this world is and how illogical it is.

Are these the same themes or material that draws you to make the kind of movies you do?

Yes, yes, the movies that I'd like to do, but the movies that I do more for the money than what the movie's got to say. But whatever, I think that whatever the movie is I try to bring something of my humaneness to the character and hopefully it makes it a better movie and at least it's entertaining. And I have common sense enough to know that in order for a movie to do any good at all, you have to first entertain.

What is your approach to acting?

I never was into any kind of method. I think that like Cagney said, "You just plant your feet, look 'em in the eye and tell 'em the truth." I think that's basically acting. I think this Method stuff is, for me, is absolute nonsense. I think acting is acting. We are acting. We are pretending. Like children pretend. Some of the best actors are children because they don't involve their ego in it. They just cast themselves wholeheartedly into having great fun. I think as an actor to just get yourself out of the way and totally involve yourself in the character you play. And know that it's acting. This Method acting, my God that must be tough on these actors. To work up the tears. You know, as an actor, if you make a face like you're gonna cry, you're gonna cry. If you hold your chin up like that, you're gonna talk like Marlon Brando. Just physical stuff you do that makes your body do things. There are techniques to acting. There are things that I use that I get myself out of a rough spot I'm in.

What are some of the techniques you use?

I have a habit if there's like I need a period, ha, ha, ha, I laugh. It gets me from one area to the other. I find myself using that as a crutch at times. So now, I let that quiet play and it's says a whole different thing. I'm still learning. We all are learning how to apply this craft of acting. I don't think it's any great art. I don't think it's anything like the great painters of the world or the great musical composers. Or Shakespeare. I don't put myself in that realm. But I think nonetheless it is an art form. But it just kills me that some of us actors, we take ourselves so seriously. Hey, man, you're just pretending. We're just being kids, you know? Don't take yourself so damn seriously, okay? When they say, "Cut," go and have some coffee and a sandwich or something. Don't think of yourself as so damn important. When I was over in the Philippines doing *Apocalypse Now* for three months all these actors were saying, "Oh, man, it's just like being in Vietnam." I wanted to bitch slap these guys. I was on a ship and I was in Vietnam. Hey, jackass. This is *not* like being in Vietnam. Those poor fuckers were getting killed over there. They were being shot at every goddamn day. They weren't working eight hours and having all the money they could spend and all the booze they could drink and all the women they could screw. These guys, their lives were on the line every freaking minute and they were sleeping in the jungle getting jungle rot and getting rained on and fired on at the same time and had to live in their own shit and in their own piss. That was Vietnam. That was an ugly fucking place. You're living in paradise and you have the balls to say this is just like Vietnam, man. You're a fucking actor! Come on. Just be grateful you're an actor and don't dare compare yourself to these guys that were dying out there. Anyway, but I digress.

I knew you were in the Navy, but I didn't know you were in Vietnam.

Yes, but let me clarify. No one I knew was fired at because I was on a ship. It was a tanker. We were coming to a Navy port in the

Joe on the set of *Iron Soldier*. Shot by Steve Thompson, © Brett Kelly.

Philippines where the hospital ships would come in. Oh, man. These poor bastards, their lives are gone at 18, 19, 17 years old. Their life is gone, man. And then, these veterans came back. They're treated much better now, but when you got out of the service, you wouldn't talk about it. You wouldn't brag about it because people would spit on you. People would shame you. People would protest you, calling you killers. It's just young men who were drafted, they had no choice. But, lots of these frickin' college kids, going to college and then their daddy's taking care of them and their life is taken care of and they have the audacity to protest against these guys when they're out there giving their lives for these kids and have no concept of the freedoms they enjoy and why they enjoy them. I'm not saying what we did going into Vietnam was right, but we were there. I think we had a helluva lot more validity being in Vietnam than we do in Iraq or Afghanistan. But it's all madness.

Here's just a sidebar. In the Civil War, the letters these kids wrote home in the Civil War are so poetic. They used words and verbiage that was Shakespearian. They were just kids. Beautiful language. Now, "Duh, winning." The language has just gone to hell. Anyway, that's something else.

What was the most dangerous situation you've been in while shooting a movie?

Only working with Bobby Z'Dar. I've had a few actresses lose it and smack me. I tell you, the biggest accidents I've had were on sets. Regular sets. Union, mainstream sets. Falling off things and getting hit with things and getting shot with what they pad that stuff with. They used to pad it with wads of paper and you got that flash and getting shot with that stuff, you know? And squibs. I tell you every time somebody tells me, "Don't worry, I've done this a thousand times before," I worry. Anytime I put on that squib jacket...make sure you got it going the right way because most of 'em are great guys and very careful. But some of 'em are very laissez faire and they're hooking up all these wires. That's your life out there. I did a movie called *Retreads* on a motorcycle, which was very, very dangerous. I think I spoke about this before. I didn't learn to ride until I got on the set. But, it's funny. I always feel, as long as that camera is running, I am totally invincible. Nothing could harm me.

The first scene I ever did was a fight with my brother. The first scene. The first time in front of a camera. This was in *The Story of Pretty Boy Floyd*. And I want to go with him and he doesn't want me to go with him and I jump him; we have a tussle. So, he said, "We'll just place you and I'll slap you and you come after me." So, he slapped me. He slapped me hard, the bastard. I hit him and I didn't know until six months later I had broken his rib, because he wasn't gonna tell me that. So, there's a lot, I think, when you do fights that aren't choreographed. I was doing *Double Blast* with a couple of karate kids, Bobby and I, and they were just these little kids. They were dangerous because they could do all these kicks and everything, but I'm a human being. They were like 9 and 10. They had been doing this since they were four. That's why they got cast. Finally, I said, "Look, that camera, you can be an inch away or two feet. I react to your kick. You don't have to..." They got the message when Bobby and I took 'em back behind the bar, so to speak. I've been fairly lucky in that I've never hurt myself where I couldn't go to work the next day. I've been very blessed with that. When that camera's rolling, you think you're invincible. So, I guess I'm blessed. Knocking on this wood, I hope we keep going.

What are your favorite types of roles to play? What are your favorite types of characters?

I love subtle comedy. I think I'd like comedy dramas. I like iconic characters like a baseball player or a cowboy. Something that's, I don't want to say man's man, but when you speak as a cowboy or as a preacher or as a baseball player you kind of speak from a platform. You're not a normal guy. I'd like to play the quiet tragedies of a normal working guy, too. You know, that depth of emotion that poor bastard has that nobody sees and how desperate and how beautiful all the goodness and ugliness it is. All

of us are walking joys and tragedies. We're all madness and sanity. We're all indefinable. I love to play the spirit of man. Every character is a character, but in that character is a man. I'd like to play that man. Not what he does, but who he is. What's that emotion that is driving him? Oh my God, a guy whose wife is cheating on him. Oh my God, the depths of despair that's gotta be. A guy who loves his wife and she is cheating on him. To play that kind of emotion. I'd love for a guy to see that who's had that experience say, "Oh man, I'm right with you. I know that." This guy understands that emotion. I like to work. I don't like these movies that are just violence for violence's sake. To me these aren't characters. These are caricatures. They're one-dimensional characters that just get stabbed and beaten or stab and beat and shoot. There's no acting there. That's all about the camera and the explosions and the special effects. You might as well put a robot in there. There's no acting that goes in there. Sly Stallone, I think, is a terrific actor, but 95% of his movies, it's all shoot 'em up. Schwarzenegger, I think, has gotten to be an excellent actor. But, you know, these action heroes, they don't really speak to any one and I don't particularly care for their movies.

What are the essential Estevez movies?

See *Soultaker*. See *PrimeMates*. *PrimeMates*, I'm very proud of. See

South of Reno. See *The Story of Pretty Boy Floyd*, the first film that I ever did. I don't have my list. *Retreads.* And see *No Code of Conduct* with my brother and Charlie. When I did *No Code of Conduct*, it was in Arizona. And when I was on the set, my brother and my nephew didn't know I was in the movie until I showed up in the movie. It was Elie Samaha, who used to own some dry cleaning stores and he remembered me and we were kids together. We used to hang out up in Laurel Canyon and he said, "If I ever get...I'm going to put you in a movie." He got to be a big producer and he put me in a movie. People said your brother finally hooked you up. No. He didn't hook me up. Elie hooked me up. I'll get home today and say I wish I would have mentioned that or mentioned that, but out of everything that's out there, there's maybe fifteen, twenty movies where I'll say this is my best work. Actually with my best work, it's not like I'm better in one movie than I am in the other, but if you do a movie where you get the proper coverage and the sound is great and everything is in focus...and usually when I say the proper coverage it's when you're doing a three-person scene and it's gonna take four or five hours just to do that. For the movies I'm used to doing, you know, if you get forty-five minutes, you're lucky. Over the shoulder, over the shoulder, master, over the shoulder and you're out of there. Also, just for kicks. See *Lucky Lady* (1975), when I was a kid, with Gene Hackman, Burt Reynolds, Liza Minnelli. That was the first big movie that I did.

That's fantastic. I didn't realize you were in a movie with Gene Hackman.

I don't think Gene Hackman did either. Jack Nicholson had just done *Easy Rider* (1969). It was kind of like that. Gene Hackman and Burt Reynolds kidnap my girlfriend and me and we had all these great adventures and then I'm driving and we get to this cantina where there's Liza Minnelli and I drop 'em off and then they let me go. And then I'm there at the premiere and I'm just beaming and I'm thinking I've made it. I'm a movie star. I get twenty-to-thirty minutes screen time with two of the biggest stars in the world. So there I am, I come on screen, I'm picking 'em up. Next scene, I'm dropping 'em off. All that interplay and all those

Flyer for Joe's plays

adventures we did were cut. So, it was like, welcome to mainstream movies. But, you know, it was a great experience and I wish I were sober. I would have remembered more of it.

They were all paid a million dollars for that picture. It was at that time the most any actors had been paid and that was the most expensive film ever made. Now it's like chump change. I think that's enough for a library. Now at least people can get a-hold of those. Oh, there's a film called *Murder in Law*. It's a little classic. I play this guy whose mother has been in France and comes home but she's absolutely a mad woman. She escapes from an insane asylum and, oh, it's just mom. And I've got the regular family and mom's killing people and trying to kill my wife. As she's, oh, you're just imagining things. But it was fun and it was made at the time when the audience gave you time to let a plot develop; now you've got to have a killing every seven pages or something. But, this was a good movie.

I think the audience has gotten so complacent, so lazy. They don't allow the movie to come to them. I remember watching an action movie with my daughter and being ashamed of myself because it was all eye-candy. It was like being on a ride. We left the theatre and what are we gonna do now? It wasn't like you watch *Casablanca* (1942) and you sit and you're gonna talk about it all night. It's like eating here at Sizzler. When you're full, you go home.

Point Dume. Bobby Z'Dar says it's the best thing I've ever done. I said to Bobby, it's the best thing he's ever done. But Bobby Z'Dar is just a freakin' great actor. Like me he's in the fourth quarter. We just entered the fourth quarter. I hope he gets recognized more as an actor with his subtleties. On his feet he's just terrific.

Of all the actors you've been in movies with, who's been the most enjoyable to work with and who's been the most difficult?

I loved Jack Palance. Back in the day when we did *The Hatfields and the McCoys* (1975). We had a meeting at the director's house the day before we started shooting and I was just about to approach Jack Palance. He was just a marvelous man's man. I was playing his son. We were doing a reading of the script and then afterwards having a little social party and I walked up to him, which was very difficult for me. I walked across the room to shake his hand and just mumbling and stumbling and he just looked at me and nodded his head and walked back across the room; it was like sixteen miles because I felt like he just gave me the kiss-off and the bum's rush. I thought, all right. Screw you. Because I always felt I had talent as an actor. The very next day with the first scene up. Jack and I, "Big

Jack," we did this scene. We did the coverage and while we're doing the scene, I didn't say anything to him. I just stayed within myself, did my work. It was only the second film I did. After we finished that scene, wrapped that scene, I just started walking back to the dressing room. Big Jack Palance comes running up behind me, puts his arm around me and says, "Hey, you're a helluva an actor, kid." I fell in love with him. I was like a puppy dog after that. Wherever he went, I went. He's having lunch; I had to sit next to him. He was great. I learned a lot about being an actor on a film set. About what you do to stake out your territory. And when you're a lead on a film, responsibility comes with that. In my later career, I learned being a lead on a film that we do have certain responsibilities to the rest of the cast and the rest of the crew.

Joe Don Baker also was terrific. I did a TV episode with him called *I Shot*—very giving actor. I was talking earlier about me wanting to change the script. I changed the script on a TV script. The director was like, "Who the fuck are you?" Joe Don Baker said, "No, I like it." He was a straight shooter, man. Good, good guy. Michael Parks, my idol. I love Michael Parks. He's a great, great actor. I think he's as good as anybody—as Brando, Dean, anybody. I think he was so underrated. He would not take shit from anybody. Anybody. He would not play the studio game, and if he would have played it he would have been a superstar. He had *Then Came Bronson*, a marvelous TV series, a great movie career. Still does. Michael Parks, I thought, was a joy. These guys and the people that I work with that I enjoy were the guys that had chutzpah. They would stand up to the man. They wouldn't compromise themselves. They wouldn't compromise the art. They weren't company men and they suffered for it. Ed Asner, same thing. I love Ed Asner. He's the actor's actor in that he's a tough guy. And I don't mean tough guy, kick your ass, but he will stand up and put his career and his backside on the line for what he believes in. I admire that because there aren't many actors that will do that. They'll just turn their heads and walk away.

I was on a set. Damian Chapa, I love. I was working with him in Texas doing *Mexican American* (2007) and he was going through some shit and he was belittling the crew and he was belittling the cast and none of the actors had any name except me and I felt it was my responsibility to challenge him. And so I purposely started a fight with Damian Chapa and we got in a real screaming match and I was acting the whole time. I wasn't really that angry, but I knew I had to do something and it was like after I did that everybody was, "Yeah, okay." He had it coming and it took the tension right out of it. But I think as an actor and as a human being you've got to speak up and you've got to speak out. I think too many actors and people that are in the public eye and have a place to say something; they just take the money and run. And they got to understand that with that position comes responsibility. My brother Martin Sheen and I are not close, but he stands up and I admire that. I've always admired that about him. Courage. And I never knew that courage can be learned and once you speak up it becomes easier. It's that old adage, pray with your hand up and not your hand out. We're here for such a short time and when you get to my age and if you've sold yourself out that's very painful to go home every night and sleep knowing that you've sold your soul. I'm human. I've done some things I shouldn't have and I should have done some things that I didn't. But, I think, overall, I stood up for myself and I'm proud of the way I handle myself; to this stage in the game anyway.

Was that the movie that you first stood up for yourself on?

That's something I've believed in all along, but that was the coup de grace where I literally staged it. If I got a problem with a cameraman or a director, I have to speak to 'em about it. I have to air it because I can't just swallow that. And I tell you something. I have never not been paid. A lot of movies I've been in, the producer has screwed some actors out of money. It happens, but it doesn't happen to me. I just will not let that happen.

What's the most difficult time you've had getting paid?

I did a movie, and I don't want to mention names. It wasn't Damian Chapa. Damian Chapa paid me. He was always great about that. But I was playing an Irishman and it was about the Irish trouble in Northern Ireland during the time of the trouble back in the '70s. I loved that movie. The lady who did it had all the money and so we didn't shoot for a year, then we picked it back up. And I had a helluva

Joe in *The Hatfields and McCoys*. Courtesy of Joe Estevez

lot of trouble getting paid the first time and she would pay me in increments. 300 here, 400 there. Finally, she paid me off and the second time when we went back I said, "I'm not gonna do this again" and she swore she would pay me and, of course, she didn't and everybody's check bounced. It was a two-week shoot. The first checks cleared and the second checks bounced. Not mine. I called her three, four times a day and I said, "No, no, you're gonna pay me." And she did. It's not that I'm a cheapskate or whatever, but I refuse to be cheated like that. You've got the money; you're going to pay me. I do a job, you're gonna pay your plumber, you're gonna pay me. It's like, well, you're an actor, it's not like real work. No. I think that's the whole dignity of the thing. It's the same thing that I made a pledge to myself about 25 years ago that I would not work for free. I would not work for free. And people said, "Well, it's a great script and it's an artistic sort of thing," and I said, "I'm happy for ya. When you get some money and you still want me, come on around. If you don't have any money, there are actors out there that would love this shot, that need this opportunity." I said, "Go for them. This is professional. You've got to pay me. If I think I can bring your film up to a certain level that costs you money. I'm worth something. You got to pay me."

I did an expo about 20 years ago where I was the emcee of it and I got stiffed. And that's the last time I got stiffed. That's not gonna happen again. They left town and I don't know their names or whatever. One guy he owed me $250. I don't want to mention his name, but I was down at the film market and I ran into him and we're all down there and he's fairly well known. Not well known, but people recognize his face and everything. We're sitting there and he said, "What are you pushing down here?" There's like about six people around and I said, "You know you owe me $250." It took a lot of courage for me to say that, but I had to say it. I humiliated him in front of these producers. He took it out of his billfold right there and paid me. And, of course, we haven't talked since, but he was just humiliated. You get some people and you only make a couple thousand dollars, oh five hundred here and three hundred here and then when it gets to, oh, they just forget about the last four or five hundred. I don't think so. Like I talked before about unions and they have their place and such, but I don't need a union to take care of me. I'll take care of myself. I'll stand up for myself. I think it's the manly thing to do. Stand up for yourself. Demand what is rightfully yours. When you don't, when you're silent, you get walked on. That's what's happening in this society. There's this old adage, this old story about this guy picketing this execution that was taking place in Texas and he's out there picketing against this man being executed, against capital punishment. A fellow said to him, "You think you're gonna change people's minds by picketing out here?" and he said, "I'm not doing this to change anybody. I just don't want to change me." He had to get out there and stand in the rain for what he believed. That's what I believe and I think if we all did it it would be a much better world because people will walk on you if you let them walk on you, so you stand up and be counted.

Do you think the film industry is shady?

I don't think it's any more shady one way or another than any other industry. You have your less than honorable people and you got your reliable people in every industry including the motion picture industry. I found the overwhelming majority, especially the independent filmmakers, I like these guys and these ladies because what they want to do is make a good film. They got something to say and they've chosen to say it in a motion picture and I'm proud that they use me as a tool to help them say that. And I'll play with them. I'm not a guild guy where it's, oh, it's eight hours and it's overtime. I try to look at the big picture and I say this guy's trying to make a motion picture. I'm gonna help him as much as I can to make this motion picture. I'm not gonna be abused. I'm not gonna work fourteen hours and do a ten-hour turnaround and come back and do another fourteen, but I'll give 'em twelve hours a day. I'll give 'em six days a week. I realize he's got limited funds and he's trying to say something. I'm not gonna be abused, but at the same time I'm not gonna take advantage of him. This is what I signed on for. Normally, I get paid pretty good and I say I'll give you a twelve-hour day and most independent films it's an eleven-hour day with a half-hour or an hour lunch and if they go over a half an hour or an hour one day it's okay. I'm okay with that. I know the guy's gotta get his shot. I know he's only got his location for one night. I know he's got to get this during the weekend. The guy's making a movie for Christ sake. I'm gonna help him finish this movie. In that sense, I'm a team player, but you pay me. Don't take advantage of me.

What would your dream role for a historical figure be?

I don't have an individual physical person that I'm dying to play and I'm too old for a baseball player. I can still play a cowboy. I think a cowboy, an old cowboy. I would love that because I think you can speak about things as a cowboy that you can't as a businessman, that type of character. But I don't want to play John Kennedy or Abraham Lincoln or Hitler. If it comes down the pike and they offer it to me I'll do my best with any role but no historical character really catches my eye. You know, I love Gandhi. Mahatma Gandhi. The Dahli Lama. I love Martin Luther King. I love historical characters and I like to play the essence of these characters and what they're saying about life and the challenges of being a human being. I would love to do that, but I don't have to be playing the Dahli Lama to say that. You can say that as every man. Speaking of the Dahli Lama, what courage. What a marvelous movie that would be; the incredible courage he's had and he's always had and he's always joyous and in love with life.

Is there any type of role you haven't been offered that you'd really like to play?

We searched forever to find a play to do over in London so I read dozens and dozens of two-hander, three-handers, two-character plays. And, frankly, the plays that I wrote, *Hobos* and *Pizza Man*, I'd like to play those guys because I wrote them. I wrote them from my heart, I wrote them from my essence. I know totally what they're about. But they're stage characters and if somebody offered to make the film, I don't know if I would because they were written for stage and for live and I don't know if they would work in a two-dimensional world, but *The Old Man, Long Day's Journey Into Night, Death of a Salesman, Night of the Iguana*: most of the characters are stage characters.

Who are you favorite playwrights, influences?

Of course, there's Eugene O'Neil, I love Richard Nash, the guy that did *The Rainmaker*. I love that character that's bigger than life. Lancaster, I think, did the movie. I did the play when I was a kid. I love Shakespeare. Oscar Wilde, my God, what a great gent. I love his sense of humor. What a marvelously beautiful and tragic character. He was marvelously flaming gay and was persecuted. It took guts to write that stuff.

How did you get yourself back into the mindset of positive thinking?

My second wife divorced me. It was probably the lowest point in my life. I had seventy bucks. That was it. I left the house with seventy bucks. I was just out on the street and living with friends and whatever. A little here, a little there. I had two kids I still had to

Headshot courtesy of Joe Estevez.

support. It was a very, very trying time. It was probably the most down, depressing time in my life because I wasn't wanted. I didn't make enough money. I was making more money than I'd ever made

in my life. That's when I was cleaning the carpet. They had a drug-
store and on the weekends I would be working 30 hours, 15 hours
a day Saturday and Sunday so I could bring myself up to do acting
work and it was a very wealthy family and I just, I wasn't making
the cut and they kicked me to the curb and I just...I was searching
for my identity and, my God, I was trying and I was just lost. So
because, first of all, you can go to the library and get stuff for free.
I didn't have any money and I was holed up in a little one-room
place in Hollywood and I got these Depaak Chopra, just these
positive...and I never thought about positive thinking one way or
another. I thought life was pretty much hit or miss and either you
were lucky or you weren't. I said, well, I had absolutely nothing to
lose and every day I would force feed myself positive thinking. I
would force feed myself and if I got a negative thought, I would just
get it out of my mind. They say if you have a thought for ten
seconds it's yours. Otherwise, it's just passing through. So I would
just get it out of my mind and reinforce it with a positive thought.
The kids that are on drugs have a saying today, fake it 'til you make
it. So, I started force feeding myself this. I started...and it was
simple. It was very difficult. It was not easy when the world is black
all around you and the wife throws you out and everybody else kind
of kicks you to the curb. So, it's like I didn't have a lot of friends. I
had a few good friends, but that's it. Because I was putting so much
energy into that marriage, very little into my acting and so I didn't
have connection or, you know, so it was just me hanging out.

So, I started this positive thinking and I was really working with
it and I was if there's something here, I'm gonna find out. I started
getting work out of the blue. I mean totally out of the blue. I got a
job that was the biggest voiceover job I got and it was in Little
Rock, Arkansas. The guy had his back to his TV and he's doing
something and *South of Reno* was on and he heard my voice. He got
the title, but I don't know who this guy is, just his character. He
wanted my voice for this campaign. So, one day I'm in this little
hole in the wall and a week later, I had this incredibly big check
from going down to Little Rock, Arkansas, and doing this string of
voice-overs for what was Broadway Bank in Texas. And I thought,
my God, and so I kept this up, this positive thinking and if you
look at from 1986 on I've worked about twice as much every year

as I had before. If not more and it wasn't connections, it wasn't me working harder. In fact, I worked harder before that. It was positive thinking. It was just positive thinking. And I got *Soultaker* during that time. I got *Retreads*, which we were in Wisconsin, and I was very much into the positive thinking. And, you know, the mosquito is a state bird up there and it's big. And everything is, all our stuff is motorcycles on location. And I just made a calm prayer to myself, to the universe, to God, that I had nothing that these mosquitoes want, these mosquitoes have nothing that I want, so we'll just live in harmony together. I just put that out in the universe, kept it as a thought. Everybody else was spraying themselves down. Everybody else was getting eaten alive. I didn't get bit by one mosquito. And it was a turning point. But not for the good. It scared me to realize I have that much power. That as a single human being, that I have that much power. I was afraid to be responsible for that power. So I've never really gotten back to being that positive because I'm afraid of knowing who the real me is and how much power I have. But, you know, it's like, wow. Because with that comes responsibility. With yourself, who you are, for the world you live in. And I wasn't ready to accept that. I think I'm more willing to accept it now because I don't have as much to lose. I'm not nearly as material now as I was then. But when you know you have that responsibility to speak up then you have to do it, to accept that responsibility. So, that was an interesting turning point and now I think I'm a pretty brave guy, but I don't know if I'd accept it. Anyway, that's as honest as I can be on that.

Have you always been spiritual?

I've always been spiritual, although I've never been as strong as I am now. I was spiritual when I was younger, but I was weak. I had an incredible sexual drive and I loved the chicks. When you're an actor and you're playing the lead in all these plays, you get a lot of chicks. And I partook as much as I reasonably could. I was a scumbag. I was married. I was weak. I was weak-willed. Now I don't have as much at my age the sexual drive of somebody in their 20s or 30s so nature has kind of...I'm not saying that's anything by self-control; nature has taken a hand. But, I know myself better; I'm able to

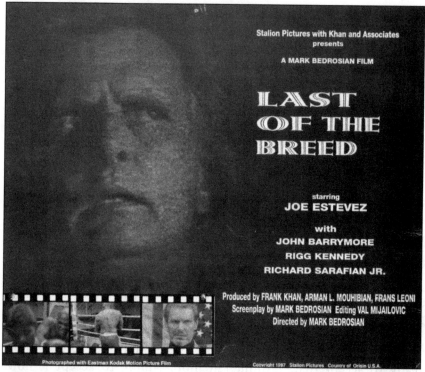

Last of the Breed. Courtesy of Joe Estevez.

accept my weaknesses. I'm able to negate my weaknesses more and accentuate my positives more. I am finally, except for being overweight a little bit, the man I always wanted to be. I always thought before I aspired, I spoke the gospel but I never practiced the gospel. Now, since I've met my lovely wife Constance, I talk the talk and I walk the walk. I've learned that life is a trip. It is a journey. And through the years, you find out more about yourself. We're like fine wines, we come to maturity and some of us are lucky enough to get to my age, to realize ourselves, who we really are. Not who we thought we are. And when we do realize who we really are, it's pretty good. I'm a pretty good guy after all. I think I said this before, in my 20s, if I could look to the future and see myself today, I'll take that. I like that guy. I could have been a drunk. I could have been a drug addict. I could have been a hen-pecked husband. I could have never even tried professional acting and stayed in the factory. So, I'm not the most courageous person in the world, but I took a lot of chances. Constance, my wife, we took a chance getting married and it's beautiful. We've grown together. We were talking about that today. Sometimes it works; we bring out the humanness in ourselves. That humanness, to have it accepted and to find I'm pretty smart. And Connie is pretty smart. All that time back in the day, I thought I was just fooling people. They'll think I'm smart, actually I'm a dumbass. But I think, no. I'm pretty smart. I'm not taking credit for it. I just take responsibility for the person God made me. Take responsibility for my smartness and when I fall short of that or half step or I take the easy way, well, I'm not being the kind of guy I should be. Anyway, I hope I answered that.

What part of you do people not see in the movies?

I remember this stripper and they said to her, "Don't you feel uncomfortable taking off your clothes in front of these men?" She said, "No. I'm not naked. Look at these men's faces. That's nakedness." So, when I am performing, I just get down to the basic instincts of me. I think I'm more me acting than I am when I'm not, because I'm totally unprotected. I am totally just vulnerable to what that fellow actor says to me or, you know. I'm just totally...I just react instinctively. While here, I've got some cover. I can't let Joe Estevez get in the way when I'm acting. I think really you watch my movies, you probably see me more than, ooh, another movie, *Together and Alone*. Duane Whitaker. Duane Whitaker said this comment, "That was the best use of Joe Estevez than any of his films." *Together and Alone*: I play an acting teacher that's trying to get one of his students. You know, the typical sleazebag acting teacher. Yeah, *Together and Alone*, it's an excellent, excellent movie. Duane Whitaker, I give him all the kudos. He wrote this puppy. He acts in it, he directed it. I played such a pathetic character. I've always disliked acting teachers. And I disliked myself when I did it. That's why I stopped. I said to the guy, you know, I can't do it anymore. I'm just done.

Was this before you were an acting teacher?

No, I was an acting teacher up the street and I didn't really teach acting. I tried to inspire these kids to be fuller human beings rather than actors. You can't teach anybody acting. And I just ran out of spiel. I can only give so many examples. I could only have so many speeches in me about how you can be a better human being or how you can trust yourself or how you can trust the tool, the energy you are. I could only find so many ways to tell these kids so then I said I had to go. This is just nonsense, this is...we left amicably. And Josh Sands and his brother Larry, great kids. I like them. They believe in this acting stuff and good for them.

I think *Together and Alone*, that was the fearful me. I don't know why actors when they cry hide their face. I do it right in the camera, man. You're gonna turn away. I'm gonna, I'm not gonna hide. If you don't want to watch this, 'cause this is tragedy, when a grown man cries. I let this pathetic character cry. When this young girl runs out and leaves him to his miserable self, his whole life is a lie. His whole life is misery. He cries. You need to show that. So, I don't...there's a...I'm pretty much what you see is what you get. When I was younger, there was a side of me, my debauchery, my cheating on my wife, my drinking, my doing drugs that I hid. That's a part I didn't want to show people, but that's all behind me. It's a good part and parcel of what makes me who I am today because I learned an incredible amount of lessons from that that make me what I am today and makes me a whole lot more understanding about poor drunks. These poor, poor people that are hooked on drugs. They got this monkey on their back. These people that just can't, sex addicts or whatever that...my heart bleeds for these people. A drunk's not a drunk because he wants to be. He wants...he's got that pain, man, that you're trying to silence. Those drugs, they become a life in and of themselves. There's a great book called *Junkie*: William Burroughs. That's what life is. Your whole life is doing junk and that's it. You'll screw your friends and everything to get that money to get that fix and that's what life has come down to. I was saved from all that. I was delivered from all that. So I can play, I know those emotions. I know those absolute depths of despair and I can play them as an actor. I've lived them. I can play them much more maturely than I could in my 20s and 30s. But I hide nothing now. It's all in the performances and there's nothing hidden. I'm the same guy here as when I'm at home. Still rattling on.

COME OUT AND PLAY!

Baby GHOST

KIDS ADVENTURE FILM ENTERTAINMENT PRESENTS
A FILM BY DONALD G. JACKSON & CO. BABY GHOST™
STARRING JOE ESTEVEZ ERIN O'BRYAN CONRAD BROOKS JAMES D. WHITWORTH
ANDY HUBBELL MARK WILLIAMS BABY GHOST SONG BY ELIZABETH MEHR
DIRECTOR OF PHOTOGRAPHY JONATHAN QUADE FILM EDITOR MATT X. LAWRENCE
WRITTEN AND CO-PRODUCED BY MARK WILLIAMS PRODUCED AND DIRECTED BY DONALD G. JACKSON

What do you think about the bad rap horror movies get?

I think horror is great. I think movies like *House of Usher* (1960).
Vincent Price. Anything that Vincent Price does. I love the *House
on Haunted Hill* (1959). I love that kind of...*Soultaker*, I love that
kind of movie. It's scary, that character. There's a guy out there
taking people's souls. There's a nether land and this land exists. Talk

to Bobby Z'Dar about when he was in a coma for two weeks. And the evils and the demons that came to visit him. They're out there. They exist. Bobby will tell you. He was in Hell. He was in Hell and he was able to come out of it. The shit that was going on in his mind while he was in a coma. These movies and I've done some of them and I'm not proud of them. There are movies that are blood and gore and I won't do those anymore. I don't think that they're entertaining. I think they appeal to the baser emotions of the human experience and I don't think those should be encouraged and that I've been in movies that I've done that, I won't say I'm ashamed of them because I didn't realize at the time the damage that I could be doing with these and my brother and my nephews and most actors have because we make a living out there. I'm in a place now hopefully where I will never have the weakness to do that again. I just did a movie with Bobby Z'Dar called *Little Creeps* where I conjure up these three demons, but they're midgets because I messed up the spell and they go out and they wreak havoc and it's fun. There's no squirting blood and axes in the eye. Just fun stuff. I like that. But I just, I don't. I look at a script, I don't even like getting blood on me. *Film noir* I've never seen one drop of blood. But now it's like it's just visual effects. It's bullshit. I don't even think these directors know what film noir is. They've never seen anything that Bogie did, any Raymond Chandler. They don't understand that wonderful experience. I did a marvelous movie with a director called James Chean which is also, put this on the list, it is called *Silent Scream*. Dana Plato's last movie, done in black and white. It has some obvious flaws and you'll see them, but I think for the most part it's a horror film, but it's a good horror film. It's got real plot and it's got real character development. He's not killing these people just to kill them. There's a reason when he's…it's madness, you know, madness. I love to play madness. I love just to say the word. Madness.

What's the most unbelievable rumor that's ever been said about you?

I have three children and a lovely wife and I've got brothers and relatives back in Ohio and I think untrue things that are said about me, I just don't...especially with the Internet and TMZ, this shit's gonna live on long after I'm dead. And it hurt me very, very much when my nephew Charlie was having troubles with *Two and a Half Men* and this guy said he was my manager and he wasn't and he said that I said that I wanted to take Charlie's place on *Two and a Half Men*, which is absolutely ludicrous. I'm in my 60s. It's absolutely ludicrous. But because I'm his uncle, TMZ just got a-hold of that and it was all over the gossip shit. He did it twice and then again and when that happened, his name is Ed Meyer. I said,

JOE ESTEVEZ

"Look. I can't have you in my life, man. That you did this." He said, "Oh, it doesn't matter what they say about you as long as they mention your name." I said, "No, I don't give a shit about that. This is me, man. You know whatever my score is on the IMDb Pro, that might go up or go down, but this is me, this shit is going to live on forever." I said, "Just, you're out of my life. Lose my telephone number. You're no longer my friend, acquaintance, anything." So that's it. And then he comes out and he's suing Charlie Sheen because Charlie wouldn't let them, let me do a reality series. I've never wanted to do a reality series. I couldn't care less. I have three people out there right now that want to do a reality series with me. I couldn't care less. I don't want to do that shit. I don't want people...I wake up in the morning or I'm sitting here talking, I don't need that. It's garbage. My God. To be that exposed. I hate that shit. But he put that out and so it said in there that Joe Estevez says his name is not attached to this lawsuit. But then, you read a couple weeks later that it is Joe Estevez suing his nephew. And Ed Meyer and all that is cut out. The headline just says, "Joe Estevez Sues Nephew." So, that made me feel really bad. Out and out it's just a frickin' lie. In this world it doesn't matter whether it's a lie or whether it's truth. If it's printed and it's out there, it's just accepted. And you have to live with it so I'm living with it, but, so I think that hurt me. And it still hurts me.

How does it affect you now?

There's nothing I can do about it. It is what it is. That's about it and for being around this long and for all the people I've had contact with and such, that's pretty good. There's nobody out there casting dispersions on me. There was that one mobster. He said he was from a crime family. There was a commercial I was going to do and this crime family guy was the producer. Jimmy Williams was also producing it. And so something else came up. I said, "Jimmy, I can't do that." He said, "Oh, that's great. We'll just get somebody else." Jimmy was just doing me a favor and then this character called. And he said, "Hey, man. You don't know who I am." I said, "I know who you are. You're a punk. You don't threaten me," and I just went off on him. I went bonkers. Unfortunately, he was recording it and he sent the recording to SAG. I don't know how in the hell he got a-hold of my brother, but he sent it there and my sister-in-law calls all scared and everything. I never told Connie this: I work in Chicago quite a bit. I worked for a young gentleman; he's a good actor, Dominic Capone. I'm convincing myself and everybody's scared and I said, "I don't think this guy's gonna do anything. He's a wild hair, you know?" Dominic said, "Don't worry about it." Last I heard from this guy. Then I get a call, I guess a month later. Then, one of his cousins or something calls and he says, "Listen. You gotta forgive my cousin. He's just a wild hair and we gotta just kinda keep him." Dominic talked to him but I didn't—I didn't want anything to do with it. But Dominic, I do owe you a favor, buddy. I work a lot in Chicago and I'm very welcome there and there's a lot of...if you're friends with that particular precinct you're in, you own that precinct. They'll shut streets down for you and that kind of stuff. Chicago's been very good to me. I haven't worked there this year, but I've worked there at least a couple of times a year. Connie's been there with me a number of times. They're always very good to us. I don't get into that mob thing. I don't owe anybody anything except Dominic, I'll do you a favor, buddy. I think, I don't know what happened, but the guy calls me later, "Oh, it's all right." So, it's all taken care of. But, that's about it. For being around this long, that's not bad.

How would you like to be remembered by people long after you're gone?

Really, I would like people to say he was a good guy. He was a damn good actor. And then he was a great guy. But he was a damn good actor. I'm sorry, it's my ego. I try my best. If I'm remembered by at least that....you know, I think people don't understand how difficult it is to give a good performance in an independent movie when there's so very little money and you get so very little coverage. And you aren't working with people that are the tops in their fields. Often you're working with students or people that haven't done this very much and they're literally learning on the job and that often times your best take isn't used. On the take that's in focus or where the sound is right which may be, you know, your third or fourth choice. But the main thing is, you get so very little coverage. If you get a close-up from about four different angles, a dead man is gonna look good. If you're talking for more than five seconds and that camera's on you, you're vulnerable. If you watch TV and even movies nowadays, count: one thousand one, one thousand two. One thousand three. Ninety percent of the time you will not get past three or four before it cuts to somebody else. If you can't do three or four seconds...but in independent films it's often you're carrying that whole damn scene in a master. They don't have time to do anything else. You ever watch a play back home? You ever watch when there's a stage play that's coming to town? And so the local newscaster, they'll show you a little scene of that stage play. And you'll look at that and you'll say, man, that sure is artificial. Well, that's an independent movie, folks. That's what we get. And you got some brilliant actors up there on stage, some great stage actors. But, when that's all you got, you're very vulnerable out there, and there's an old adage with doing independent films. I don't want any flies on me.

What does the phrase, "I don't want any flies on me," mean?

If I'm gonna save myself in this scene, I'm gonna turn that other actor around. I've heard a lot, "You know that film sucked, but you were pretty good." It's not an accident. I've rewritten the script. I'm trying my best not to get any flies on me. A lot of actors don't even know it exists. It's this great undiscovered jewel to the mainstream people that the only real movies available are the ones that have three thousand theatre releases. There is an incredible amount of gifted filmmakers out there, brilliant, that see how to tell a story in film with a unique and different kind of angle. Literally and figuratively. And they apply this art, making a film. I think filmmaking is much more deserving of being an art form than acting. I'm just a tool. But to be able to make this marvelous little...if you see Duane Whitaker's *Together and Alone*, it's a minor masterpiece. The guy had no money at all. He put this together with blood, sweat and tears. It's a marvelous, marvelous film. I mean, he's got a real talent and just to come after this story to have the balls to shoot it in black and white. I admire these guys. I admire these new filmmakers. And all of them try. Most all of them try. And some fall short of the mark, but it wasn't for lack of trying. And maybe their next film like Tarantino said, his first film was his film school. See, people like that make me sick.

Why does Tarantino make you sick?

Here's a guy with incredible freakin' talent, man. And he makes *Grindhouse* (2007) and this violent shit. And I know that's what makes the money, but give us a piece of art, man. Because you got the talent. God's given you the talent to talk through film. Get some balls and chutzpah, man. Give us something that speaks to the heart of man. To the compassion to the spirit of man that can raise us above ourselves. We were talking about Don Maclean the other day that we're gonna see in April coming to town. This guy's a great, marvelous poet. This guy's brilliant. He's a wordsmith and my God. The images that he can paint with his words is just marvelous. The images that Tarantino can paint with his film is just marvelous, but he chooses to appeal to the lower instincts of man.

Shame on him. Fuck him. That's not what moviemaking should be about. That's using the great talents God gave you to make money, not to make a difference. We're given these talents to make a difference. To make the plight of man a little bit better. We're artists. That's what our obligation is here, not to make all the money we can and hide out in Malibu; let the rest of the world go to hell in a hand basket. We're supposed to be in there with it in the muck and the mire and to help change things. These guys aren't doing it. Instead of trying to solve the problems, they become the problems. They become the man. *Raging Bull* (1980), I'm sorry, I know it's a great film, I think it's pornography. I really do. I think he's a guy with a great talent and to show this violence for violence's sake, what the hell did I get walking away from *Raging Bull?* How much better am I after walking away from *Raging Bull?* What does that, how does that feed my spirit? You see *Doonby*, you're gonna walk away with something that's gonna make you think. That's gonna make you rise above your normal way of thinking. That's what movies are about. Whether you agree with the thing or not, that's what movies are about: to stimulate you, to make you think, to make you take action. But just to sit there and watch this pornography. To add to the rest of the violence in the world and think that that's the way that the world speaks that's through this violence and to think that that's how kids are influenced is through this violence. Marvelous cinematic violence. It's fucking marvelous cinematic garbage. To take those talents and to do that with them, man, you've got to answer for that. You've got to answer for that.

If Charlie has tiger blood what kind of blood does Joe Estevez have?

Joe Estevez is a pussycat. I am the gentlest, easiest man in the world. Let me say this: I have never hit another man in anger. I've hit people by accident, doing movies and things. Even as a kid, I've never. I know I'm not answering the question, but I am. I've always pictured a human being as the temple of the human spirit. And I was telling Connie that as a kid, I got the shit beat out of me more than once, but that I didn't fight back because I couldn't hit that person. I joined the Navy because I knew if I was drafted into the Army and had to fight in Vietnam I would be killed because if I had to shoot another man I couldn't do it because I couldn't see that man as the enemy or as a gook or a Vietcong. I saw him as just as another human being as myself. So, I don't piss tiger blood, I piss cat's milk. I'm a pussycat.

Courtesy of Joe Estevez.

AND BABY MAKES THREE
BY JOE ESTEVEZ

In Hollywood I'm known as an independent film actor. That means I work on "indie" films which not very many people see, for a lot less money than the mainstream actors make. But don't think you'll ever hear me complain. It's a great life. I'm an actor, which is the only thing I ever wanted to be. I work a lot, and if I do say so myself, I'm pretty good at it.

Commercial acting, on the other hand, is another world altogether. What it takes to be a success at that, I really don't know. Either you've got it, or you don't. In over thirty years as a professional actor I've done maybe, four. Of course, that's not a great average, but still, once or twice a month, my agent calls with a commercial audition. If I am available, I go, because—well, you never know.

About a year ago, I got an audition for a China commercial to be shot in Hong Kong. I went, not because I actually thought I'd get the job but more to keep my agent happy and I did not want to offend the "great acting karma god"....well, they loved me, which is always a bad sign. Commercial actors will tell you when they think they gave a really poor audition somehow their chances are better for getting the part. I know, it's crazy!

Anyway, a week later, the phone rings—and I got the gig. No callbacks, no nothin'. Just "Here's the money offered, here's the date you leave for Hong Kong, take it or leave it." Of course, I took it.

Now, on overseas flights, I know it's first come first serve on the seat arrangements (they flew me economy, of course). So I got to the airport early and got the bulkhead window seat (almost like first-class) that I wanted. The flight was a "3" on a 1 to 10 scale of misery. Not bad at all for thirteen and a half hours in the air.

It was a five-day job. First day, travel and wardrobe. Three-day shoot. Last day, "pick-ups," if needed, and fly back home. I was taken to wardrobe right from the airport. An hour, tops, I thought, then I'd get plenty of rest for the next day's filming. After over five hours of trying on different combinations of outfits, I got to my hotel room only to be called back one half hour later because the client didn't like the director's choice. Three hours later, I'm finally in bed hoping to get four hours sleep before the next day's call.

Now, I always thought of myself as a pretty tough guy. Not tough like I'm gonna beat anybody up, but I pride myself in that I could hang with the best of them. I've worked long hours doing physically difficult stuff for some pretty rough task masters and left the set with the respect of the cast and crew—of course, that was before I worked in China! When they said, "three days shooting," they meant three eighteen-hour days. All actors stayed on the set at all times just in case we were needed. One half-hour lunch (when time permitted), no trailer to rest in, not even your own chair. Air-conditioning was a fan they used in between shots to try to bring the temperature down to ninety degrees. No glamour here, folks, no little make-up missy fussing over me on this set. My costume was a white suit (with pants too tight), white shirt, shined shoes and it was my responsibility to keep myself looking sharp. They expected perfection and worked until they got it. I'll say this, though, these guys are fair. They treated this Yankee no better or worse than anybody else— and I hate it when that happens! I have great respect for those film-makers in Hong Kong, but given a choice, I'd think twice about going back. You call me a sissy? That's fine. Quite frankly, I just don't like working that hard.

After three days of shooting, we still had a short scene to do on my travel day. When we finally did wrap, my plane was leaving in five hours. They offered to take me back to the hotel for a nap, but I opted to pick up my luggage and go straight to the airport. I wanted to get there early to get my favorite bulkhead window seat (almost like first-class). On the flight back, I could get plenty of rest. I was dog-tired, bone-tired. Places I didn't know I had were tired, but there I was first in line waiting for the ticket booth to open—it did—finally—and I got my cherished seat.

Now, I don't drink, carouse, or do drugs but I do smoke cigars and in the Hong Kong airport, stuck way back in the corner, is an Irish pub. Yeah, I know, an Irish pub in Hong Kong. Go figure, huh! In that Irish pub I was pleased to find out I could smoke. And smoke I did. Two big long fat ones back to back while I waited the four hours for my flight. I smoked and mused over the past four days, I thanked God for the gig and I really thanked God that it was over.

I don't understand why people stand in line waiting to board a flight. We are all going to get there at the same time, so why sit an extra thirty minutes or so in that plane seat if I don't have to? I make it a point to be the last in line—or almost as there is always a few people who think like me, but not this time. After getting that last puff and reeking of cigar smoke I was the last customer on board. I headed back to that bulkhead window seat (almost like first-class) that I treasured so much. Everyone was already seated except for this family of three. Mom, Dad and the kid. They were putting their belongings into the overhead compartment and settling into my row and Ho! Wait a minute—settling into my seat! As I stood there waiting for them to discover their obvious mistake, the stewardess approached me to ask a small favor but not before oogling and cooing to the baby and telling the parents how beautiful the kid was. Then, as if she were sure I'd say yes, she explained loud enough for all the passengers to hear, that the family wanted to sit together and would I mind changing seats with Dad. "Well, where is Dad sitting?" I asked. She pointed to the middle seat, in the middle row, in the middle of the plane. I looked, and there it was, or at least about the four inches I could see of it. The two adjoining seats were occupied by a couple of Sumo wrestler-type guys whose ample girth spilled over generously in all directions. While I'm standing there contemplating my answer it seemed every steward and passenger took turns telling Mom what a beautiful baby she had and what a charming family the three of them made.

Like I said, I'm a pretty tough (although fair) kind of guy who stands up for myself when my back is against the wall. Here I am, as tired as I've ever been in my life, working three days without sleep, sacrificing a nap to get to the airport four hours early to get this seat, so I can give it up to this guy who's probably been on vacation, slept in and got to the airport late. Like, this yuppie expects some poor sap (i.e. me) to gladly give up his seat so his cute little family can sit together. All eyes, and I mean, ALL eyes are on me, and all ears are attuned. These folks are getting a little early in-flight entertainment. They can all watch this stooge, me, the schlep, melt under the social pressure, pretending I couldn't be happier getting screwed out of my seat. "Yes, of course," I'm supposed to say, "I don't mind a bit, I'd be delighted." Then, they get to watch me slink back to the shittiest seat on the plane as I try to convince myself I'm a Good Samaritan, but I know I just got the royal shaft and for the next fourteen hours I'm going to suffer for it—I DON'T THINK SO! Trust me, it took a lot of courage, but I felt I was standing up for every poor dope who's ever been put in this position. Okay—that's a lie. I just wanted my seat—I earned it. So, with as much understanding as I could muster in my voice, under the circumstance, I said "I'm sorry, no." Maybe hate is too strong a word here, but I felt a very strong dislike from every person on that plane, especially the stewards. No extra bag of peanuts for me, that's for sure!

As I crossed to my window seat (easily, of course, because of the extra leg room) I murmured a quick "I'm sorry" to the mom as I passed. "I understand," she said, you know, I believe she was one of the few people on the plane who really did understand. I liked her for that and for some reason then, I felt kind of sad.

As we buckled up and got ready to take off, Mom was busy taking care of her little boy. She was so gentle with him. Almost too gentle. She was a big woman and every move was an effort. He would drop something or other and it took her forever to pick it up, clean it off and give it back to him so he could throw it on the floor again. "This isn't going to last," I thought. "In a few minutes, when everyone quits paying attention to the kid, she'll strap him tight to his seat and whisper in his ear to shut up and quit jerking around or he's going to have hell to pay when she gets him alone," but she didn't. She was so attentive to him, so caring, as if the slightest wrong move and the kid would break.

Let me stop right here and tell you something from my heart. I couldn't help myself, I really liked this lady. I'm going to try not to sound corny, but I'll just tell you this because it's true. The woman looked like my dearly departed mother. Not just looked like her but smelled like her. Moved like her. Sounded like her—okay, I'm going to leave this right here. Maybe she'll be another story of mine down the road but for now just let me say a guy's only got one mom and I wouldn't compare her to just anybody—so I'm telling you, this lady was special.

My favorite part of flying or should I say, the only thing I like about flying, is taking off and landing. I love to watch the city, especially at night, fade into the clouds and coming out of the clouds heading home. I like to watch everything get bigger and bigger. I'm a kid like that. Well, when we were finally off the ground, and my head's gawking out the window, the baby, the little baby wraps his whole hand around my finger. Me, the guy who banished his old man to the abyss of in-flight misery. The kid didn't realize he was giving the prick sitting next to him a little bit of unconditional love. I felt weird, like I was getting affection under false pretenses. I didn't want to turn around and look at the baby because—because I didn't want him to let go of my hand. Only when we were well into the clouds did I turn to look. There was Mom, who was looking at the kid holding my finger. Then, for the first time, I looked at the boy. Really looked at him.

Have you ever had a time in your life that something became clear to you that for the longest time had been clear to everyone else? Like sitting at a green light and wondering why the hell everybody was blowing their horn. There was this beautiful young boy, straight black hair, narrow eyes, big round face—and Chinese. Obviously Chinese. There I was, the last person on this plane to know Mom and Dad went to Hong Kong to adopt this child. They hardly knew the little guy and this trip was the first real time they were spending together.

Long after the folks aboard forget this flight, they will still have a vague dislike for anyone who smells like cigar smoke. They won't remember why, but I will. I was thinking of those Southwest Airline commercials—"Need to get away?" You bet, but "duh!"—I'm already on the damn plane. Needless to say as discreetly and quickly as possible, I traded seats with the dad. As I expected, the next thirteen hours were some of the most miserable hours of my life, and I felt great.

SPECIAL THANKS

BRAD PAULSON:
To my mother and father for their constant love and support as I've pursued endeavors and a career outside the path of the normal and the sane. To Chris Watson for his friendship and for being such a fun collaborator. He is truly a kindred spirit. To Andrew Rausch, a true appreciator and supporter of independent cinema, and might I add, a fantastic writer. And to the subject of our book, Joe Estevez: a superb actor, wonderful human being and one of the greatest friends a filmmaker could ask for.

CHRIS WATSON:
This book wouldn't be possible without the assistance of the great Joe Estevez. Joe is truly one of the nicest people I've ever met and one of the few actors I'm comfortable suggesting to filmmakers. This book was a quick, last-minute project made easier by the help of several people. First, a huge thank you to my cohort on the project, Brad Paulson, for making the book as quick and fun as possible. Second, I must thank Dr. Scott Shaw for taking the time to share some memories about Joe for the introduction. Dr. Shaw is a true artist who consistently surprises me by his willingness to help out— I owe him numerous times over now. Third, I must thank all the kind filmmakers who donated photos: Scott Shaw, Adrian Carr, Mike Tristano, Dave Campfield, Brian Wilson, Blake Fitzpatrick, Ron Marchini, producers of *Bunyan*, and Brett Kelly. Fourth, thanks to the friends of Joe who helped us start the book off with some comments about him: Duane Whitaker, Conrad Brooks, Robert Z'Dar, Jay Richardson, David Heavener, and Richard Norton.

Also, it's important to acknowledge the publisher of this book. Ben Ohmart is the reason we were able to do this project. His patience with our over-eagerness and odd fetishes is much appreciated. Last, but not least, a huge thank you to Drew Martin for designing the cover for the book.

ABOUT THE AUTHORS

Brad was born in Glasgow, Montana, and attended Montana State University, where he received his bachelor's degree in film/video. He's been in love with movies ever since he was a little kid and saw *Superman II* at a friend's house and stayed glued to the TV while his friends went outside and played. Little did he know moving to Los Angeles would not only result him in meeting the great Joe Estevez but also having the pleasure of directing him in his own films. Co-writing a book about the man, the myth, the legend that is Joe Estevez has been a dream come true for Paulson. This is his second book, the first being *Dwarfsploitation* also with Chris Watson. Brad currently lives in Los Angeles, California.

Chris Watson is an award-winning filmmaker of several internationally distributed films. Watson previously co-wrote the books *Reflections on Blaxploitation, Dwarfsploitation,* and *Dirty Talk*. Watson has also written for *Inside Kung-Fu Magazine, Paracinema Magazine, B-Independent, Strictly Splatter, East Side Boxing* and numerous other magazines and websites.

INDEX

CPSIA information can be obtained
at www.ICGtesting.com
Printed in the USA
FSHW022104240720
71718FS